BUILT IN AMERICA
LIGHTHOUSES
A CLOSE-UP LOOK

BY THE EDITORS AT FOX CHAPEL PUBLISHING

FOREWORD BY BOB TRAPANI,
EXECUTIVE DIRECTOR, AMERICAN LIGHTHOUSE FOUNDATION

BUILT IN AMERICA
LIGHTHOUSES
A CLOSE-UP LOOK

BY THE EDITORS AT FOX CHAPEL PUBLISHING

FOREWORD BY BOB TRAPANI,
EXECUTIVE DIRECTOR, AMERICAN LIGHTHOUSE FOUNDATION

FOX CHAPEL
PUBLISHING

© 2011 by Fox Chapel Publishing Company, Inc., East Petersburg, PA
Foreword © 2011 by Bob Trapani
All art courtesy HABS/HAER Website unless otherwise noted.
"Built In America" series trademark of Fox Chapel Publishing

Lighthouses is an original work, first published in 2011 by Fox Chapel Publishing Company, Inc.

Front cover photo courtesy of Mark Comstock. Back cover photo courtesy of Jeff Rozema.

Architectural drawings and black-and-white photographs courtesy of the Historic American Building
Survey and the Historic American Engineering Record, Library of Congress. Color photographs courtesy of
Kraig Anderson of www.lighthousefriends.com, Mark Comstock, Jeff Rozema, the Pensacola Lighthouse
Association, and the National Park Service.

ISBN 978-1-56523-560-1

Library of Congress Cataloging-in-Publication Data

Lighthouses / by the editors at Fox Chapel Publishing ; with a foreword by Bob Trapani. -- 1st ed.
     p. cm. -- (Built in America)
  Includes index.
  ISBN 978-1-56523-560-1
  1. Lighthouses--United States. 2. Lighthouses--United States--Pictorial works. 3. United States--History,
Local. 4. United States--History, Local--Pictorial works. I. Fox Chapel Publishing.
  VK1023.L525 2011
  627'.9220973--dc22
                          2010051390

To learn more about the other great books from Fox Chapel Publishing, or to find a retailer near
you, call toll free 800-457-9112 or visit us at *www.FoxChapelPublishing.com*.

Note to Authors: We are always looking for talented authors to write new books.
Please send a brief letter describing your idea to
Acquisition Editor, 1970 Broad Street, East Petersburg, PA 17520.

Printed in China
First printing: June 2011

CONTENTS

About HABS and HAER

The Historic American Building Survey (HABS) was created in 1933 in an effort to preserve and document the country's architectural history. The program's creation came at a time when preservation efforts were being undertaken across the country. It was during the same period that the Williamsburg colonial capital was being restored and the National Park Service was working to establish historical parks and National Historic Sites.

HABS was to become a part of these early preservation efforts by continuing the work of individual architects across the country. Architects who had an interest in the past, particularly the colonial era, often took steps to preserve some of the architectural history of that time period by compiling drawings and photographs of historic structures. Without the funds or backing of a large program, however, these efforts were sporadic and often centered around the areas in which the architects lived.

Since its founding, HABS has worked to bring this architectural documentation to a national level. Formed by the American Institute of Architects, the Library of Congress, and the National Park Service, HABS collects and documents a wide range of architectural resources from across the country. In an effort to provide a complete understanding of the nation's architectural history, the HABS collection includes well-known structures designed by famous architects, along with a variety of structures that reflect the building traditions of their local communities.

The Historic American Engineering Record (HAER), established in 1969, grew out of a connection formed between HABS and the Smithsonian Institution's Museum of History and Technology (now titled the Museum of American History). HAER, formed by the National Park Service, the American Society of Civil Engineers, and the Library of Congress, became the means of documenting sites and structures that were historically important to the development of engineering and industry.

HAER is instrumental in documenting structures such as bridges, ships, steel works, railroads, and canals. While HABS focuses on documenting architectural style and design, HAER seeks to preserve an understanding of the internal workings of the machinery found within historic buildings. Most recently, this has meant a thorough documentation of maritime structures.

The preservation efforts of both HABS and HAER have allowed this book to come together as a compilation of the wealth of historic information the two programs have documented.

Since its founding, HABS has helped document architecture from the colonial period, such as the house pictured here, as well as countless other architectural styles.

FOREWORD

Americans are fascinated with lighthouses for many reasons, but perhaps none greater than the hope and strength that these majestic structures continue to embody.

Just a glance at a lighthouse can affect even the most casual observer, leading to an understanding that these buildings stand for much more than their apparent value as historic structures. Their distinctive appearance speaks to vigilance and service to others and to unsurpassed engineering excellence in their design.

When it comes to the importance and role of lighthouses in our nation's history, it can be argued that no other single non-military asset has been of more value to its people and their prosperity than the lighthouse. While lighthouses are usually thought of in relation to guiding ships, it was actually American commerce that inspired the financing, construction, and maintenance of the beacons.

In order for the country's commerce to flourish, America had to demonstrate a courageous and industrious spirit and establish a shipping industry that could effectively transport and safely deliver a host of goods.

As history has pointed out time and again, lighthouses allowed America's maritime commerce to grow into a powerful industry by guiding ships filled with precious cargo into the bays and harbors of the country's coastline.

Before the days of railroads and trains, and later macadam highways and trucks, waterways were the nation's "highways." American ports, from Boston to New York and Philadelphia to Charleston, received everything from important overseas imports to coastal trade goods, which included staples such as food, lumber, and ice. As a network of lighthouses and other aids to navigation proliferated along the country's coastal waterways and rivers, the nation saw a similar growth in commerce, prosperity, and military strength.

For all their stately beauty, lighthouses would have been completely ineffective were it not for the powerful lights that shone from the tops of their towers. Most American lighthouses were lit using the Fresnel lens, invented by French physicist Augustin Fresnel in the early 1820s. The Fresnel lens uses a system of highly polished glass prisms arranged within a brass assembly to reflect and refract light, creating a beacon of unparalleled brilliance. The prisms in a Fresnel lens produced such a concentrated beam of light that it could be seen farther out to sea than any lens used previously, ensuring that sailors had a much better chance of avoiding navigational hazards.

FRESNEL ORDERS

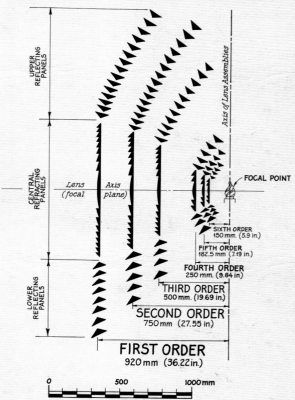

The Fresnel lens, invented by French physicist Augustin Fresnel, consists of a central light surrounded by hundreds of glass prisms, which concentrate the light into a narrow beam. The "order" of a Fresnel lens is determined by its focal length. Orders one through three have the largest focal lengths and can therefore project light the farthest. They are most often used in towers located along a seacoast. Orders four through six have the smallest focal lengths and are typically used in lighthouses located along rivers, bays, or harbors.

COMPARATIVE TABLE OF LENS ORDERS

ORIGINAL FRESNEL ORDERS		OIL CONSUMPTION PER HOUR		RELATIVE BRIGHTNESS (6th ORDER=1)	MODERN LENS ORDERS (U.S.A.)	FOCAL LENGTH		HEIGHT OF COMPONENTS								APPROXIMATE WEIGHT OF ASSEMBLED LENS		USE
ORDER	N° OF LAMP WICKS	gm.	oz.			mm.	in.	LOWER REFLECTOR		CENTRAL REFRACTOR		UPPER REFLECTOR		TOTAL		kg.	lbs.	
								mm.	in.	mm.	in.	mm.	in.	mm.	in.			
1st	4	750	26.25	17.69	1st	920	36.22	539	21.22	980	38.58	1001	39.40	2590	101.97	5800	12,800	LARGEST SEACOAST LIGHTS
2nd	3	500	17.5	11.54	2nd	750	27.55	378	14.88	854	33.62	810	31.89	2069	81.46	1600	3,530	GREAT LAKES LIGHTHOUSES, SEACOASTS ISLANDS, SOUNDS
3rd LARGE	2	200	7	3.85	3rd	500	19.69	278	10.94	660	25.98	593	23.35	1576	62.05	900	1,985	SEACOAST, SOUNDS RIVER ENTRY, BAYS, CHANNELS, RANGE LIGHTS
3rd SMALL	1	150	5.25	2.31	4th	250	9.84	144	5.67	300	11.81	358	14.09	722	28.43	200 TO 300	440 TO 660	SHOALS, REEFS, HARBOR LIGHTS, ISLANDS IN RIVERS AND HARBORS
4th LARGE	2	90	3.15	1.23	5th	1825	7.19	105	4.13	226	8.90	196	7.72	541	21.30	120 TO 200	265 TO 440	BREAKWATERS RIVER LIGHTS CHANNEL, SMALL ISLANDS IN SOUNDS.
4th SMALL	1	90	3.15	1	6th	150	5.9	84	3.31	180	7.09	157	6.18	433	17.05	100	220	PIER OR BREAKWATER LIGHTS IN HARBORS.

This revolutionary invention proved so effective that the scientific principal Fresnel used to create the lens is still utilized today in the development of many modern acrylic lenses.

Despite its unparalleled capabilities, the Fresnel lens was not the single element responsible for a lighthouse's effectiveness. Prior to advances in automation technologies, the lifesaving powers of a lighthouse—rooted in the efficiency of its light and fog signal—would not work without a human element.

Lighthouse keepers and their families endured much in the way of sacrifice, isolation, loneliness, and sometimes even tragedy, to care for the lighthouses and keep their lanterns lit. This unflagging devotion allowed the keeper and his light to forge a time-honored place in American history.

Countless efforts have been made to document the history and heritage of America's lighthouses. This book is a part of that effort. By immersing yourself in this remarkable volume, you will get a fascinating glimpse of the golden age of lighthouses in America. *Built in America: Lighthouses* utilizes an intriguing array of facts and photos from the collections of the Historic American Building Survey (HABS) and the Historic American Engineering Record (HAER) to introduce the important facets of our lighthouse heritage.

Rich with historic detail, the photos and drawings from the HABS/HAER collection reveal the ingenuity, craftsmanship, pride, and spirit of boundless achievement that inspired the architects, engineers, and builders of American lighthouses.

The images, which prove to be windows into the past, also show the stark reality of lighthouses pushed to the brink of oblivion by the unchecked forces of storm, neglect, vandalism, and other natural disasters. Fortunately, the HABS/HAER collection has captured an intimate visual documentation of a few lost lighthouse sites, allowing the memory of these once-proud sentinels to shine on, even if the structures themselves have slipped away.

When you next gaze upon a lighthouse, let its beauty captivate you, then do one more thing before you leave—take an extra moment to peer a little closer at its dress of brick, iron, or wood. The exquisite detail will speak to your heart and mind in a silent but unmistakable language that can forever enrich your view and appreciation for some of America's most incredible structures.

We will not see the likes of our lighthouses built ever again, so seek to understand the importance of their preservation, and keep the flame of their benevolent heritage burning bright forevermore in your hearts.

—Bob Trapani
Executive Director,
American Lighthouse Foundation

ABOUT THE AUTHOR

Bob Trapani has been a part of the preservation and documentation of lighthouses and their history for many years. In the past, he has served as director for the Maine Lighthouse Museum, president for the Delaware River & Bay Lighthouse Foundation, executive director for the Delaware Seashore Preservation Foundation, and vice president for the American Lighthouse Coordinating Committee. He currently serves as the executive director for the American Lighthouse Foundation, a national nonprofit lighthouse preservation and education organization based in Rockland, Maine. Mr. Trapani is also the author of four books on lighthouses. Mr. Trapani's wife, Ann-Marie, works with him on his current writing and photography projects, which can be seen on the website Storm Heroes or on their blog, Moments in Maine. Mr. Trapani currently resides in Camden, Maine, with his wife and their three children, Nina-Marie, Katrina, and Dominic.

9

Boon Island Lighthouse (left) and Prospect Harbor Light (below) are both lighthouses that have been documented by HABS and are now under the care of the American Lighthouse Foundation.

CAPE HATTERAS LIGHTHOUSE

DARE COUNTY, NORTH CAROLINA
ORIGINAL LIGHTHOUSE BUILT IN 1803

Under construction from 1869 to 1870, the Cape Hatteras Lighthouse is one of the most important structures on the East Coast. The light is used to guide ships through a treacherous area off of Cape Hatteras known as the Graveyard of the Atlantic. It is here that the Gulf Stream connects with the inshore current, pushing ships toward the Diamond Shoals, a dangerous sandbar that extends 12 miles in length. The original Cape Hatteras tower was completed in 1803, but due to poor maintenance and the adverse effects of the weather, a new tower had to be built in 1870. In 1873, the lighthouse was painted with its

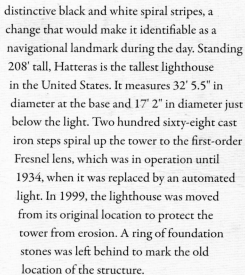

distinctive black and white spiral stripes, a change that would make it identifiable as a navigational landmark during the day. Standing 208' tall, Hatteras is the tallest lighthouse in the United States. It measures 32' 5.5" in diameter at the base and 17' 2" in diameter just below the light. Two hundred sixty-eight cast iron steps spiral up the tower to the first-order Fresnel lens, which was in operation until 1934, when it was replaced by an automated light. In 1999, the lighthouse was moved from its original location to protect the tower from erosion. A ring of foundation stones was left behind to mark the old location of the structure.

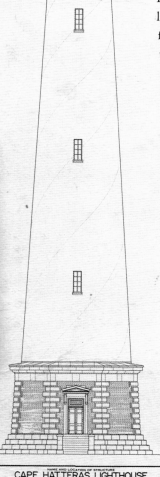

NORTH ELEVATION

CAPE HATTERAS NATIONAL SEASHORE
1989
NATIONAL PARK SERVICE
UNITED STATES DEPARTMENT OF THE INTERIOR

BUXTON

NAME AND LOCATION OF STRUCTURE
CAPE HATTERAS LIGHTHOUSE
DARE COUNTY

NORTH CAROLINA

SURVEY NO.
NC-357

HISTORIC AMERICAN
BUILDINGS SURVEY
SHEET 1 OF 13 SHEETS

Cape Hatteras, one of the most famous lighthouses on the East Coast, was built to protect ships from an area known as the Graveyard of the Atlantic.

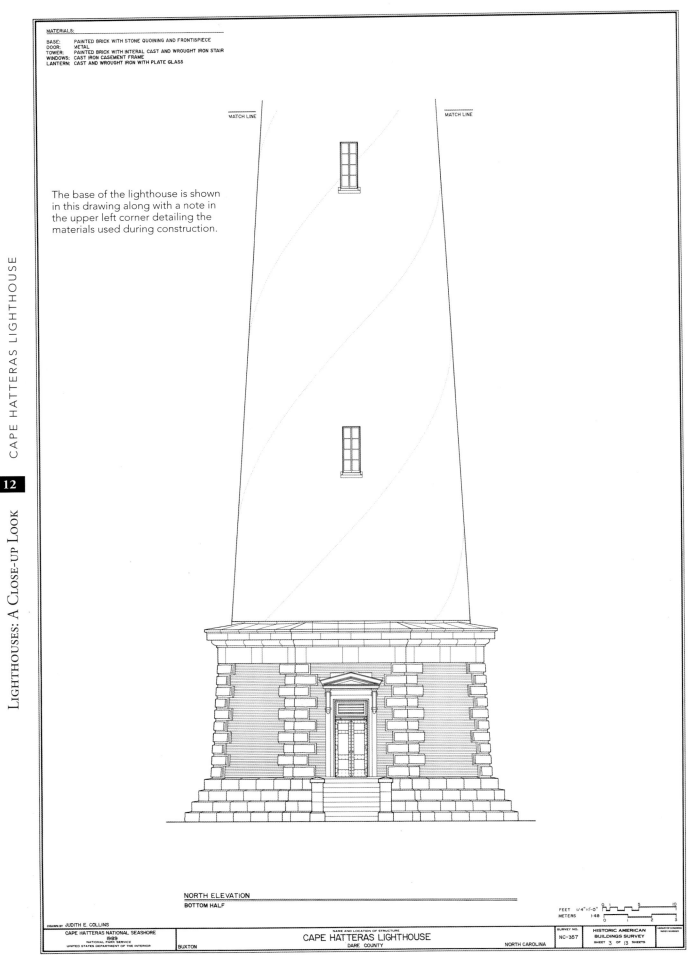

MATERIALS:

BASE: PAINTED BRICK WITH STONE QUOINING AND FRONTISPIECE
DOOR: METAL
TOWER: PAINTED BRICK WITH INTERAL CAST AND WROUGHT IRON STAIR
WINDOWS: CAST IRON CASEMENT FRAME
LANTERN: CAST AND WROUGHT IRON WITH PLATE GLASS

The base of the lighthouse is shown in this drawing along with a note in the upper left corner detailing the materials used during construction.

MATCH LINE   MATCH LINE

NORTH ELEVATION
BOTTOM HALF

FEET 1/4"=1'-0"
METERS 1:48

DRAWN BY JUDITH E. COLLINS

CAPE HATTERAS NATIONAL SEASHORE
1989
NATIONAL PARK SERVICE
UNITED STATES DEPARTMENT OF THE INTERIOR

BUXTON

NAME AND LOCATION OF STRUCTURE
CAPE HATTERAS LIGHTHOUSE
DARE COUNTY   NORTH CAROLINA

SURVEY NO.
NC-357

HISTORIC AMERICAN
BUILDINGS SURVEY
SHEET 3 OF 13 SHEETS

LIBRARY OF CONGRESS
INDEX NUMBER

The original Cape Hatteras Lighthouse was built in 1803, but was poorly maintained. The current tower, constructed with brick and stone, was completed in 1870.

13

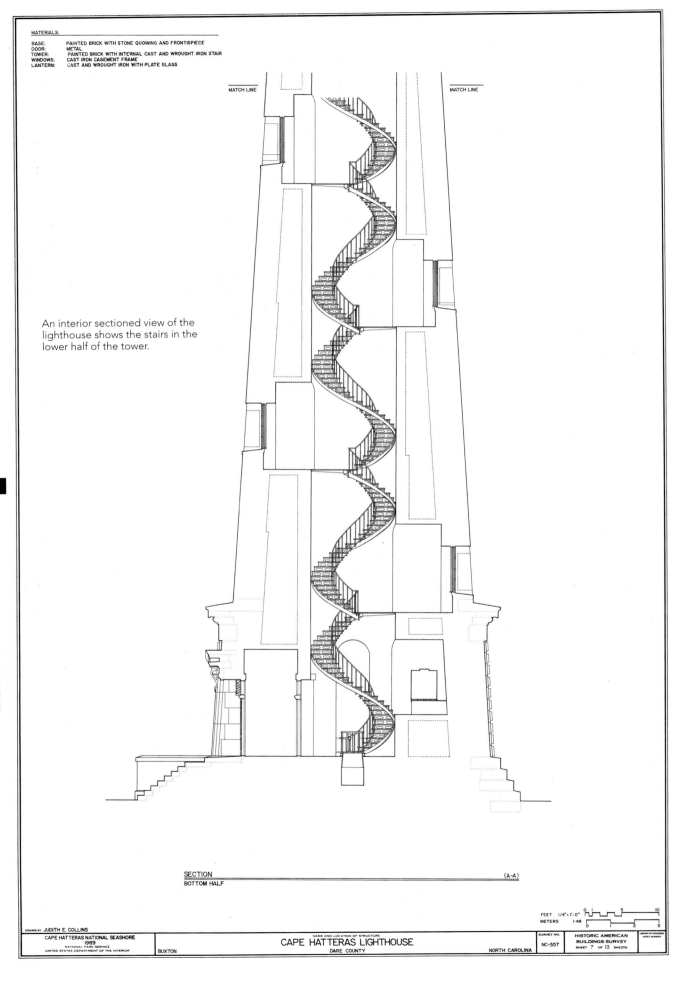

MATERIALS:

BASE: PAINTED BRICK WITH STONE QUOINING AND FRONTISPIECE
DOOR: METAL
TOWER: PAINTED BRICK WITH INTERNAL CAST AND WROUGHT IRON STAIR
WINDOWS: CAST IRON CASEMENT FRAME
LANTERN: CAST AND WROUGHT IRON WITH PLATE GLASS

MATCH LINE   MATCH LINE

An interior sectioned view of the lighthouse shows the stairs in the lower half of the tower.

SECTION   (A-A)
BOTTOM HALF

FEET 1/4"=1'-0"   0   1   5   10
METERS 1:48   0   1   2   3

DRAWN BY JUDITH E. COLLINS

CAPE HATTERAS NATIONAL SEASHORE
1989
NATIONAL PARK SERVICE
UNITED STATES DEPARTMENT OF THE INTERIOR   BUXTON

NAME AND LOCATION OF STRUCTURE
CAPE HATTERAS LIGHTHOUSE
DARE COUNTY   NORTH CAROLINA

SURVEY NO.
NC-357

HISTORIC AMERICAN
BUILDINGS SURVEY
SHEET 7 OF 13 SHEETS

HABS NO. NC-357-15

Cape Hatteras
contains 268 stairs
made of cast iron.

HABS NO. NC-357-18

Cape Hatteras is the tallest lighthouse in the United States, standing 208' tall.

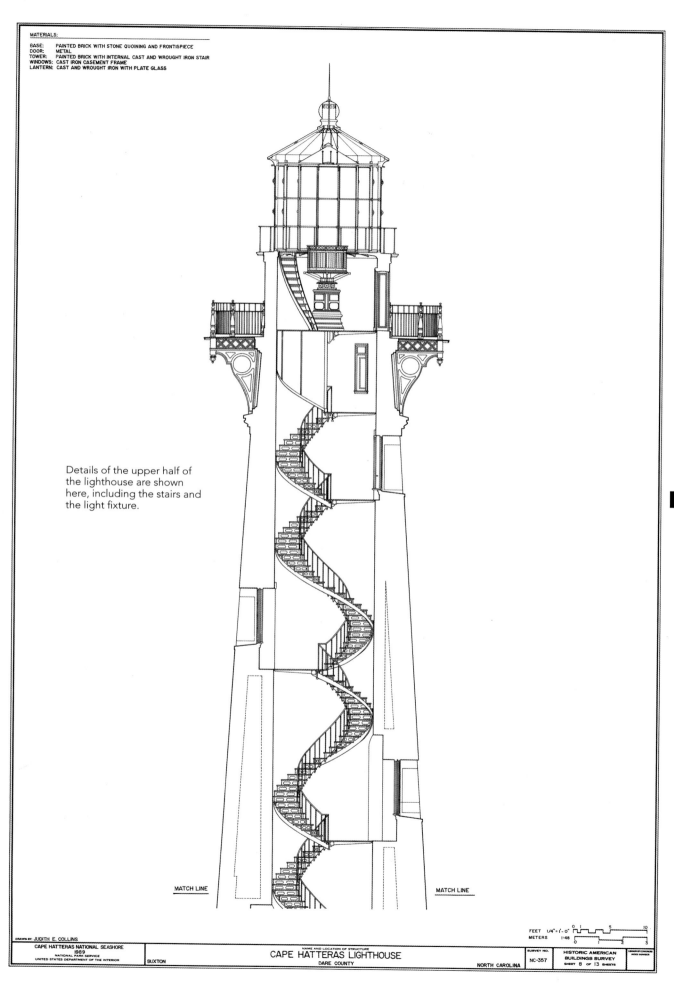

MATERIALS:

BASE: PAINTED BRICK WITH STONE QUOINING AND FRONTISPIECE
DOOR: METAL
TOWER: PAINTED BRICK WITH INTERNAL CAST AND WROUGHT IRON STAIR
WINDOWS: CAST IRON CASEMENT FRAME
LANTERN: CAST AND WROUGHT IRON WITH PLATE GLASS

Details of the upper half of
the lighthouse are shown
here, including the stairs and
the light fixture.

MATCH LINE   MATCH LINE

DRAWN BY: JUDITH E. COLLINS

CAPE HATTERAS NATIONAL SEASHORE
1989
NATIONAL PARK SERVICE
UNITED STATES DEPARTMENT OF THE INTERIOR   BUXTON

NAME AND LOCATION OF STRUCTURE
CAPE HATTERAS LIGHTHOUSE
DARE COUNTY

NORTH CAROLINA

SURVEY NO.
NC-357

HISTORIC AMERICAN
BUILDINGS SURVEY
SHEET 8 OF 13 SHEETS

FEET 1/4"=1'-0"   0 1   5   10
METERS 1:48   0   1   2   3

In 1873, the Cape Hatteras lighthouse was painted with spiraling white and black stripes so sailors could use it as a landmark not only at night when the light was activated, but during the day as well.

MATERIALS:

BASE: PAINTED BRICK WITH STONE QUOINING AND FRONTISPIECE
DOOR: METAL
TOWER: PAINTED BRICK WITH INTERNAL CAST AND WROUGHT IRON STAIR
WINDOWS: CAST IRON CASEMENT FRAME
LANTERN: CAST AND WROUGHT IRON WITH PLATE GLASS

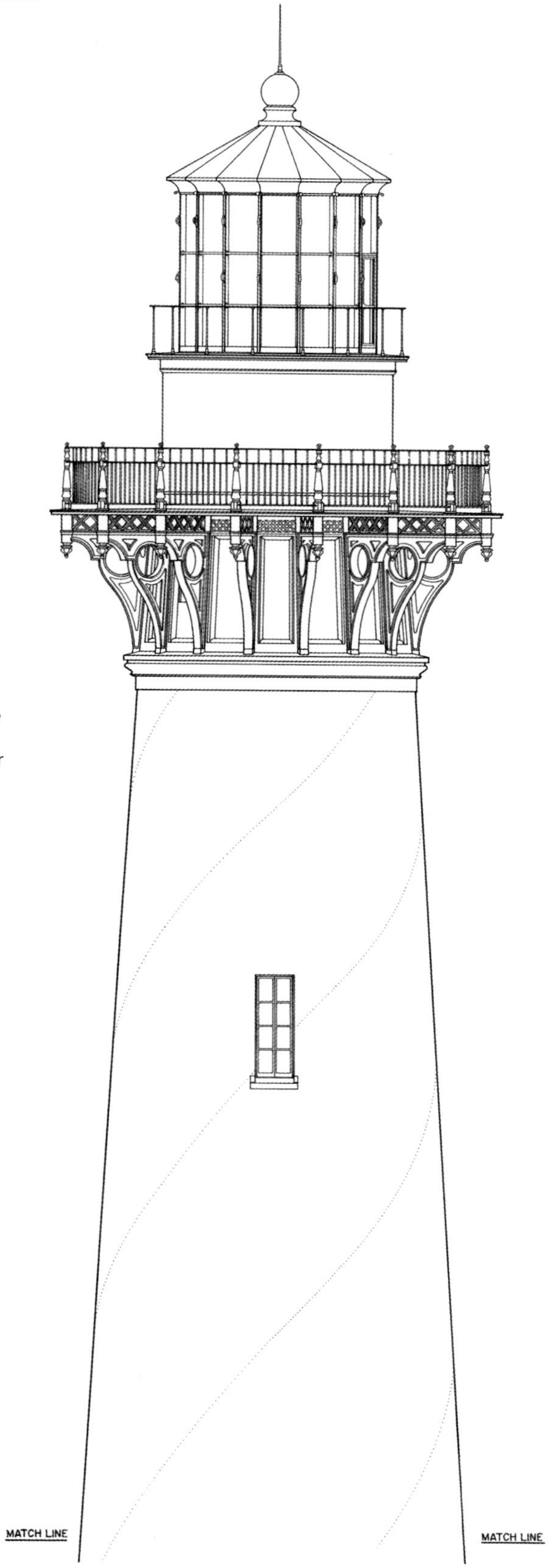

The upper half of the Cape Hatteras lighthouse is shown here with a note about the materials used for construction in the upper left corner.

MATCH LINE   MATCH LINE

NORTH ELEVATION
TOP HALF

FEET 1/4" = 1'-0"   0   1   5   10
METERS   1:48   0   1   2   3

DRAWN BY: JUDITH E. COLLINS

CAPE HATTERAS NATIONAL SEASHORE
1989
NATIONAL PARK SERVICE
UNITED STATES DEPARTMENT OF THE INTERIOR

BUXTON

NAME AND LOCATION OF STRUCTURE
CAPE HATTERAS LIGHTHOUSE
DARE COUNTY

NORTH CAROLINA

SURVEY NO.
NC-357

HISTORIC AMERICAN
BUILDINGS SURVEY
SHEET 4 OF 13 SHEETS

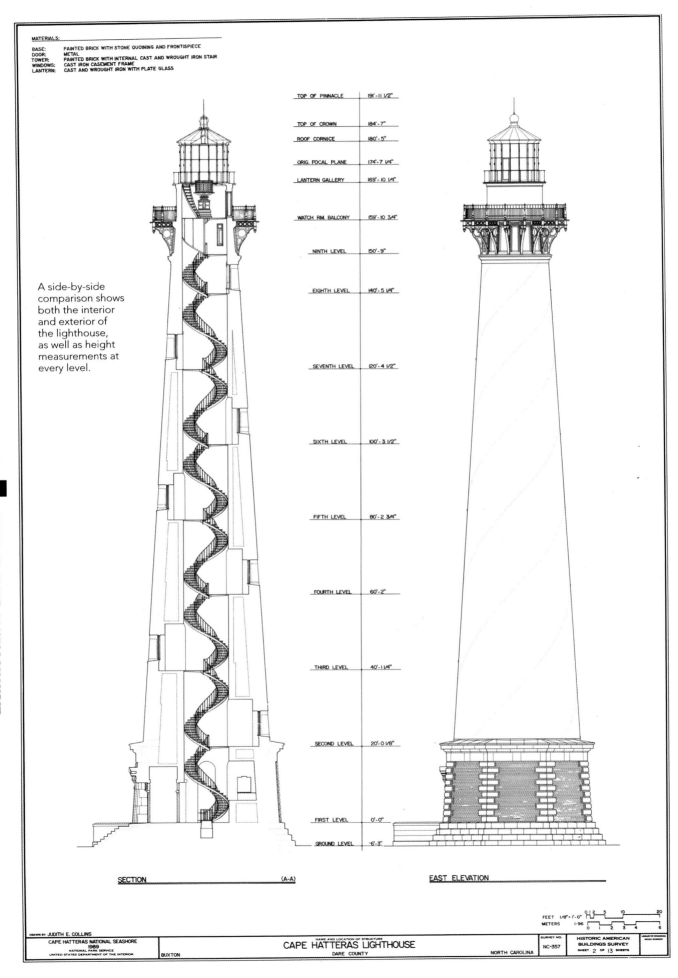

MATERIALS:
BASE: PAINTED BRICK WITH STONE QUOINING AND FRONTISPIECE
DOOR: METAL
TOWER: PAINTED BRICK WITH INTERNAL CAST AND WROUGHT IRON STAIR
WINDOWS: CAST IRON CASEMENT FRAME
LANTERN: CAST AND WROUGHT IRON WITH PLATE GLASS

A side-by-side comparison shows both the interior and exterior of the lighthouse, as well as height measurements at every level.

TOP OF PINNACLE — 191'-11 1/2"
TOP OF CROWN — 184'-7"
ROOF CORNICE — 180'-5"
ORIG. FOCAL PLANE — 174'-7 1/4"
LANTERN GALLERY — 169'-10 1/4"
WATCH RM. BALCONY — 159'-10 3/4"
NINTH LEVEL — 150'-9"
EIGHTH LEVEL — 140'-5 1/4"
SEVENTH LEVEL — 120'-4 1/2"
SIXTH LEVEL — 100'-3 1/2"
FIFTH LEVEL — 80'-2 3/4"
FOURTH LEVEL — 60'-2"
THIRD LEVEL — 40'-11 1/4"
SECOND LEVEL — 20'-0 1/8"
FIRST LEVEL — 0'-0"
GROUND LEVEL — -6'-3"

SECTION   (A-A)

EAST ELEVATION

FEET 1/8" = 1'-0"   0 1 2   5   10   20
METERS 1:96   0 1 2 3 4   6

DRAWN BY: JUDITH E. COLLINS

CAPE HATTERAS NATIONAL SEASHORE
1989
NATIONAL PARK SERVICE
UNITED STATES DEPARTMENT OF THE INTERIOR   BUXTON

NAME AND LOCATION OF STRUCTURE
CAPE HATTERAS LIGHTHOUSE
DARE COUNTY   NORTH CAROLINA

SURVEY NO.
NC-357

HISTORIC AMERICAN
BUILDINGS SURVEY
SHEET 2 OF 13 SHEETS

This sectional elevation shows the top of the Cape Hatteras tower, including the room that contained the mechanism used to turn the lighthouse's first-order Fresnel lens and the glass-paneled room that contained the lens itself.

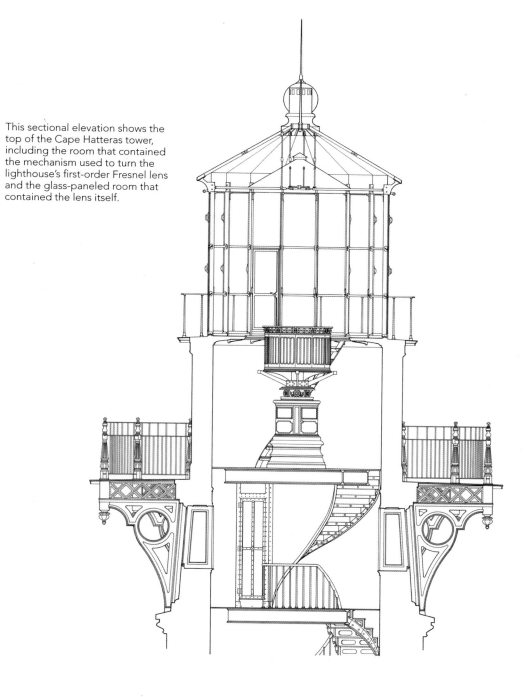

LANTERN SECTION   (LS)

DRAWN BY: JUDITH E. COLLINS

CAPE HATTERAS NATIONAL SEASHORE
1989
NATIONAL PARK SERVICE
UNITED STATES DEPARTMENT OF THE INTERIOR

BUXTON

NAME AND LOCATION OF STRUCTURE
CAPE HATTERAS LIGHTHOUSE
DARE COUNTY

NORTH CAROLINA

SURVEY NO.
NC-357

HISTORIC AMERICAN
BUILDINGS SURVEY
SHEET 13 OF 13 SHEETS

LIBRARY OF CONGRESS
INDEX NUMBER

FEET 1/2"=1'-0"   0   1   2   3   4   5

CENTIMETERS 1:24   0   50   100   150

Until the light was automated in 1934, Cape Hatteras
Lighthouse contained a first-order Fresnel lens.

HABS no. NC-357-20

A first-order lens is the largest of
the Fresnel lenses, having a focal
length of about 36".

23

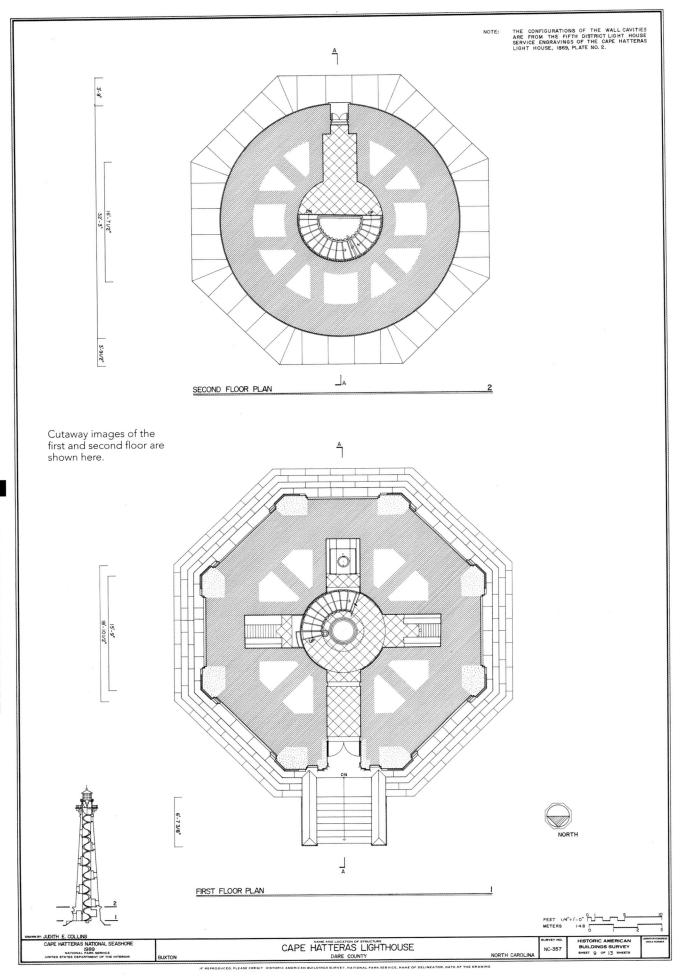

NOTE: THE CONFIGURATIONS OF THE WALL CAVITIES ARE FROM THE FIFTH DISTRICT LIGHT HOUSE SERVICE ENGRAVINGS OF THE CAPE HATTERAS LIGHT HOUSE, 1869, PLATE NO. 2.

SECOND FLOOR PLAN   2

Cutaway images of the first and second floor are shown here.

FIRST FLOOR PLAN   1

NORTH

FEET 1/4"=1'-0"
METERS 1:48

DRAWN BY: JUDITH E. COLLINS
CAPE HATTERAS NATIONAL SEASHORE
1989
NATIONAL PARK SERVICE
UNITED STATES DEPARTMENT OF THE INTERIOR

BUXTON

NAME AND LOCATION OF STRUCTURE
CAPE HATTERAS LIGHTHOUSE
DARE COUNTY

NORTH CAROLINA

SURVEY NO.
NC-357

HISTORIC AMERICAN
BUILDINGS SURVEY
SHEET 9 OF 13 SHEETS

IF REPRODUCED, PLEASE CREDIT: HISTORIC AMERICAN BUILDINGS SURVEY, NATIONAL PARK SERVICE, NAME OF DELINEATOR, DATE OF THE DRAWING

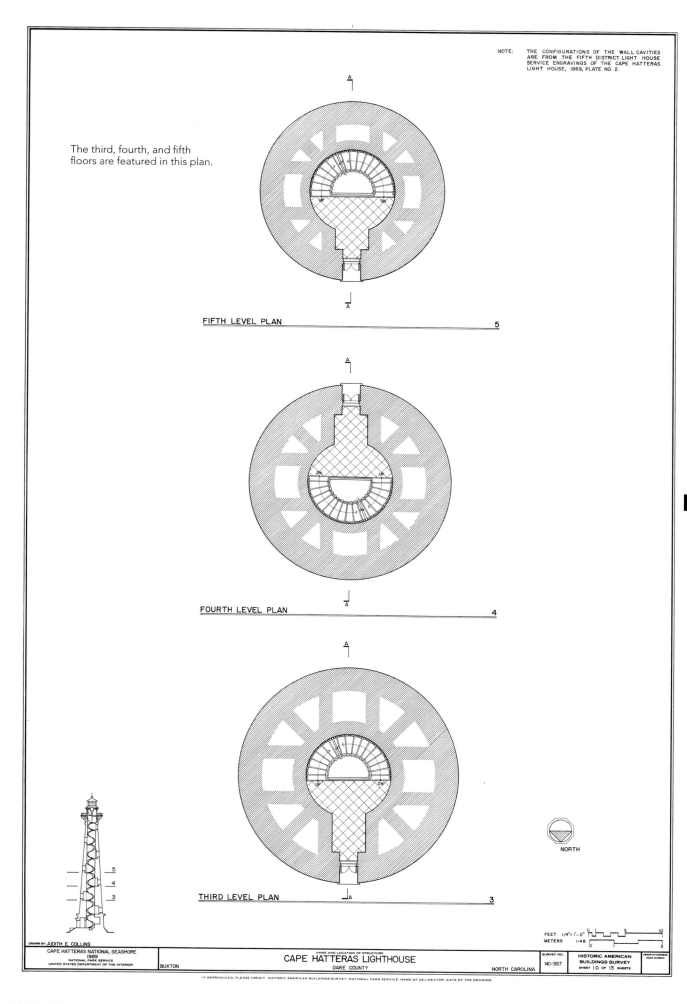

NOTE: THE CONFIGURATIONS OF THE WALL CAVITIES ARE FROM THE FIFTH DISTRICT LIGHT HOUSE SERVICE ENGRAVINGS OF THE CAPE HATTERAS LIGHT HOUSE, 1869, PLATE NO. 2.

The third, fourth, and fifth floors are featured in this plan.

FIFTH LEVEL PLAN   5

FOURTH LEVEL PLAN   4

THIRD LEVEL PLAN   3

NORTH

FEET 1/4"= 1'-0"
METERS 1:48

DRAWN BY: JUDITH E. COLLINS
CAPE HATTERAS NATIONAL SEASHORE
1989
NATIONAL PARK SERVICE
UNITED STATES DEPARTMENT OF THE INTERIOR

BUXTON

NAME AND LOCATION OF STRUCTURE
CAPE HATTERAS LIGHTHOUSE
DARE COUNTY

NORTH CAROLINA

SURVEY NO.
NC-357

HISTORIC AMERICAN
BUILDINGS SURVEY
SHEET 10 OF 13 SHEETS

IF REPRODUCED, PLEASE CREDIT HISTORIC AMERICAN BUILDINGS SURVEY, NATIONAL PARK SERVICE, NAME OF DELINEATOR, DATE OF THE DRAWING

NOTE: THE CONFIGURATIONS OF THE WALL CAVITIES ARE FROM THE FIFTH DISTRICT LIGHT HOUSE SERVICE ENGRAVINGS OF THE CAPE HATTERAS LIGHT HOUSE, 1869, PLATE NO. 2.

Levels six, seven, and eight are shown here.

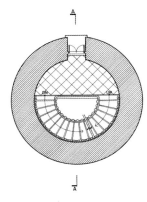

EIGHTH LEVEL PLAN   8

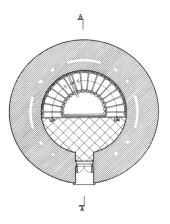

SEVENTH LEVEL PLAN   7

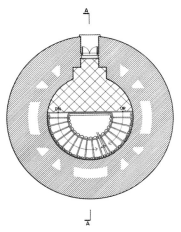

SIXTH LEVEL PLAN   6

NORTH

FEET   1/4"=1'-0"   0   5   10
METERS   1:48   0   1   2   3

DRAWN BY: JUDITH E. COLLINS

CAPE HATTERAS NATIONAL SEASHORE
1989
NATIONAL PARK SERVICE
UNITED STATES DEPARTMENT OF THE INTERIOR

NAME AND LOCATION OF STRUCTURE
CAPE HATTERAS LIGHTHOUSE
DARE COUNTY

BUXTON   NORTH CAROLINA

SURVEY NO.
NC-357

HISTORIC AMERICAN
BUILDINGS SURVEY
SHEET 11 OF 13 SHEETS

LIBRARY OF CONGRESS
INDEX NUMBER

This plan details the final three levels of the 208'-tall tower.

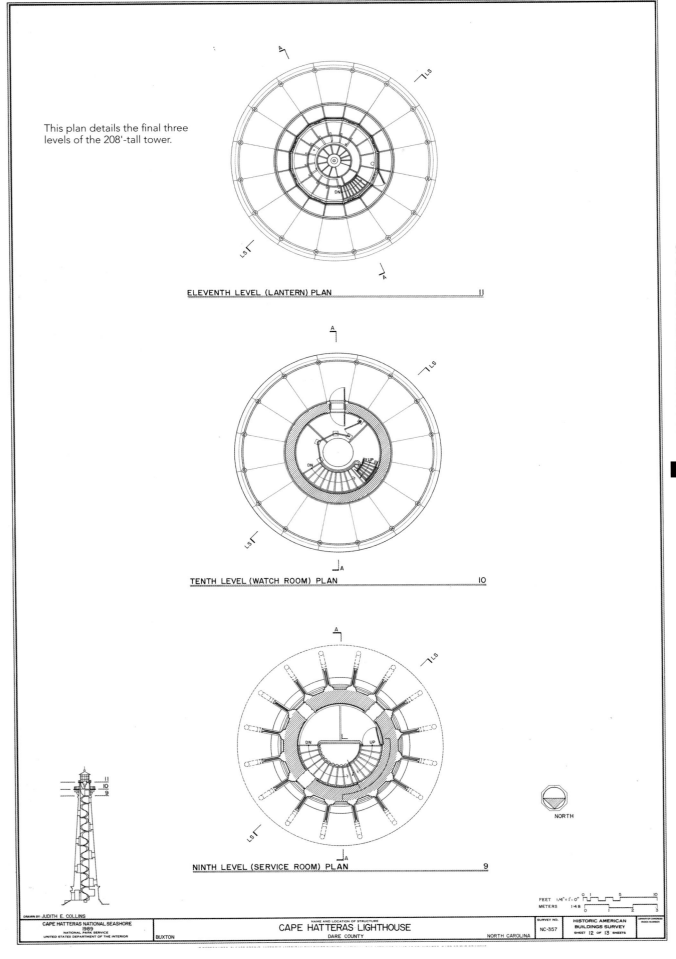

ELEVENTH LEVEL (LANTERN) PLAN   11

TENTH LEVEL (WATCH ROOM) PLAN   10

NINTH LEVEL (SERVICE ROOM) PLAN   9

NORTH

FEET 1/4"=1'-0"
METERS 1:48

DRAWN BY: JUDITH E. COLLINS

CAPE HATTERAS NATIONAL SEASHORE
1989
NATIONAL PARK SERVICE
UNITED STATES DEPARTMENT OF THE INTERIOR

BUXTON

NAME AND LOCATION OF STRUCTURE
CAPE HATTERAS LIGHTHOUSE
DARE COUNTY

NORTH CAROLINA

SURVEY NO.
NC-357

HISTORIC AMERICAN
BUILDINGS SURVEY
SHEET 12 OF 13 SHEETS

LIBRARY OF CONGRESS
INDEX NUMBER

28

In 1999, the Cape Hatteras Lighthouse was moved to a new site about half a mile away from its original location. The move, made to protect the lighthouse from erosion, took an entire month, because the tower could be moved only 5' at a time.

Mark Comstock

A ring of stones from the lighthouse foundation was left at the original site of the Hatteras light. They were later engraved with the names of the keepers who spent years servicing the lighthouse.

Mark Comstock

LIGHTHOUSES: A CLOSE-UP LOOK

CAPE ST. GEORGE LIGHTHOUSE

FRANKLIN COUNTY, FLORIDA
ORIGINAL LIGHTHOUSE BUILT IN 1833

The Cape St. George Lighthouse was built on Little St. George Island to aid ships travelling around the coast of Florida. Three towers were built on the island, the first two falling due to the extreme effects of strong winds and seas. A third tower was erected in 1852. Unlike the previous two towers, it was built farther inland and was constructed with deep-driven pilings in the hopes that its distance from the shore and strong foundation would protect it from the weather. The third tower survived the Civil War—although its light was extinguished to prevent Union ships from using it to navigate—and remained standing until the 1990s, when a series of hurricanes struck Little St. George Island. Hurricane Andrew washed away a great portion of the beach surrounding the lighthouse in 1992. Fearing that the light could no longer be used due to its tenuous position, the United States Coast Guard deactivated it in 1994. In 1995, Hurricane Opal moved the lighthouse off its foundation, causing it to lean. Through the efforts of the Cape St. George Lighthouse Society, a new foundation was completed in 2002, but eventually storms and erosion led to the lighthouse's collapse into the Gulf of Mexico in 2005. The lighthouse pieces were salvaged, however, and the original architectural plans were used to rebuild the tower on St. George Island in 2008.

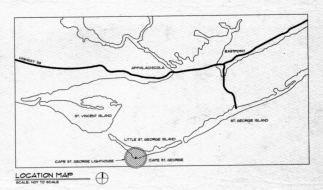

LOCATION MAP
SCALE: NOT TO SCALE

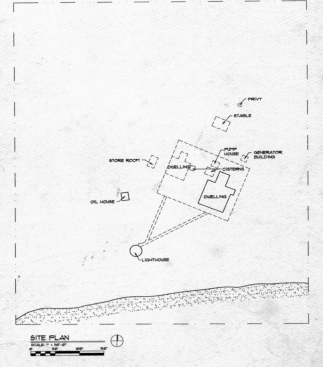

SITE PLAN
SCALE: 1" = 50'-0"

30

DRAWN BY: TONI L. GRIMES

CAPE ST. GEORGE LIGHTHOUSE SURVEY
NATIONAL PARK SERVICE
UNITED STATES DEPARTMENT OF THE INTERIOR

CAPE ST. GEORGE LIGHTHOUSE

CAPE ST. GEORGE   LITTLE ST. GEORGE ISLAND   FRANKLIN COUNTY   FLORIDA   FL-406

SURVEY NO.

HISTORIC AMERICAN BUILDINGS SURVEY
SHEET 1 OF 04 SHEETS

Three lighthouses were built at the Cape St. George site, and all three were destroyed because of the extreme effects of the weather. The third tower, pictured here, started to lean after Hurricane Opal struck Little St. George Island in 1995.

The details in this section show the elevation of various levels of the lighthouse.

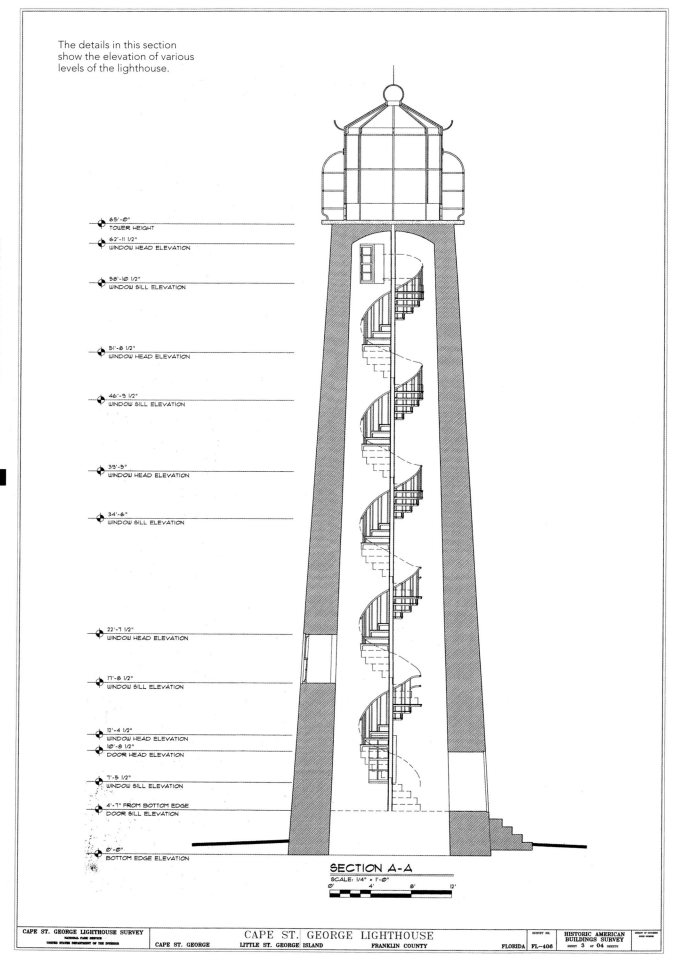

65'-0"
TOWER HEIGHT

62'-11 1/2"
WINDOW HEAD ELEVATION

58'-10 1/2"
WINDOW SILL ELEVATION

51'-8 1/2"
WINDOW HEAD ELEVATION

46'-9 1/2"
WINDOW SILL ELEVATION

39'-3"
WINDOW HEAD ELEVATION

34'-6"
WINDOW SILL ELEVATION

22'-7 1/2"
WINDOW HEAD ELEVATION

17'-8 1/2"
WINDOW SILL ELEVATION

12'-4 1/2"
WINDOW HEAD ELEVATION

10'-8 1/2"
DOOR HEAD ELEVATION

7'-5 1/2"
WINDOW SILL ELEVATION

4'-7" FROM BOTTOM EDGE
DOOR SILL ELEVATION

0'-0"
BOTTOM EDGE ELEVATION

SECTION A-A
SCALE: 1/4" = 1'-0"

0'   4'   8'   12'

CAPE ST. GEORGE LIGHTHOUSE SURVEY	CAPE ST. GEORGE LIGHTHOUSE			SURVEY NO.	HISTORIC AMERICAN BUILDINGS SURVEY
NATIONAL PARK SERVICE UNITED STATES DEPARTMENT OF THE INTERIOR	CAPE ST. GEORGE	LITTLE ST. GEORGE ISLAND	FRANKLIN COUNTY	FLORIDA	FL-406	SHEET 3 OF 04 SHEETS

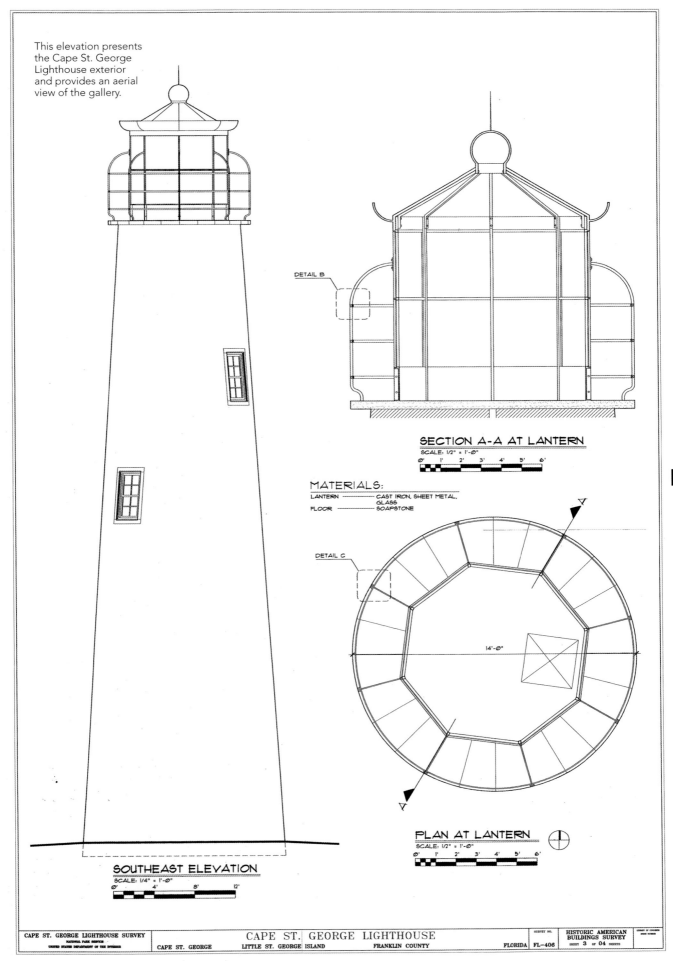

This elevation presents the Cape St. George Lighthouse exterior and provides an aerial view of the gallery.

DETAIL B

SECTION A-A AT LANTERN
SCALE: 1/2" = 1'-0"
0' 1' 2' 3' 4' 5' 6'

MATERIALS:
LANTERN ——————— CAST IRON, SHEET METAL, GLASS
FLOOR ——————— SOAPSTONE

DETAIL C

14'-0"

PLAN AT LANTERN
SCALE: 1/2" = 1'-0"
0' 1' 2' 3' 4' 5' 6'

SOUTHEAST ELEVATION
SCALE: 1/4" = 1'-0"
0' 4' 8' 12'

CAPE ST. GEORGE LIGHTHOUSE SURVEY
NATIONAL PARK SERVICE
UNITED STATES DEPARTMENT OF THE INTERIOR

CAPE ST. GEORGE LIGHTHOUSE

CAPE ST. GEORGE   LITTLE ST. GEORGE ISLAND   FRANKLIN COUNTY   FLORIDA | FL-406

SURVEY NO.
HISTORIC AMERICAN BUILDINGS SURVEY
SHEET 3 OF 04 SHEETS

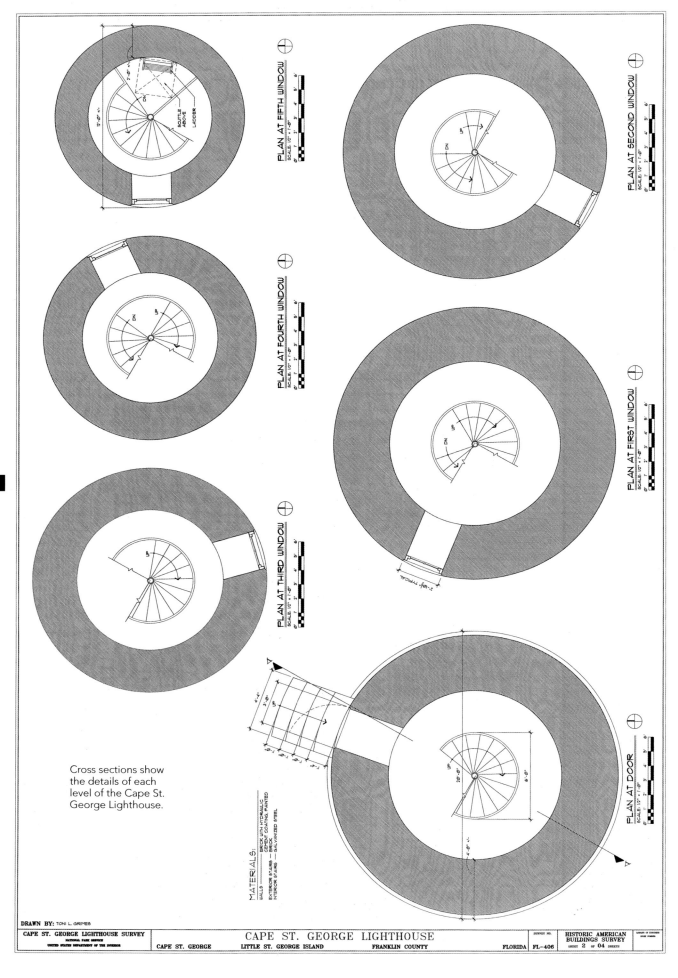

Cross sections show the details of each level of the Cape St. George Lighthouse.

PLAN AT FIFTH WINDOW
SCALE: 1/2" = 1'-0"

PLAN AT SECOND WINDOW
SCALE: 1/2" = 1'-0"

PLAN AT FOURTH WINDOW
SCALE: 1/2" = 1'-0"

PLAN AT FIRST WINDOW
SCALE: 1/2" = 1'-0"

PLAN AT THIRD WINDOW
SCALE: 1/2" = 1'-0"

PLAN AT DOOR
SCALE: 1/2" = 1'-0"

MATERIALS:
WALLS ——— BRICK WITH HYDRAULIC CEMENT COATING, PAINTED
EXTERIOR STAIRS ——— BRICK
INTERIOR STAIRS ——— GALVANIZED STEEL

DRAWN BY: TONI L. GRIMES

CAPE ST. GEORGE LIGHTHOUSE SURVEY
NATIONAL PARK SERVICE
UNITED STATES DEPARTMENT OF THE INTERIOR

CAPE ST. GEORGE LIGHTHOUSE
CAPE ST. GEORGE   LITTLE ST. GEORGE ISLAND   FRANKLIN COUNTY   FLORIDA FL—406

SURVEY NO.
HISTORIC AMERICAN BUILDINGS SURVEY
SHEET 2 OF 04 SHEETS

The Cape St. George Lighthouse Society worked to counteract the effects of the hurricane by building a new foundation for the lighthouse.

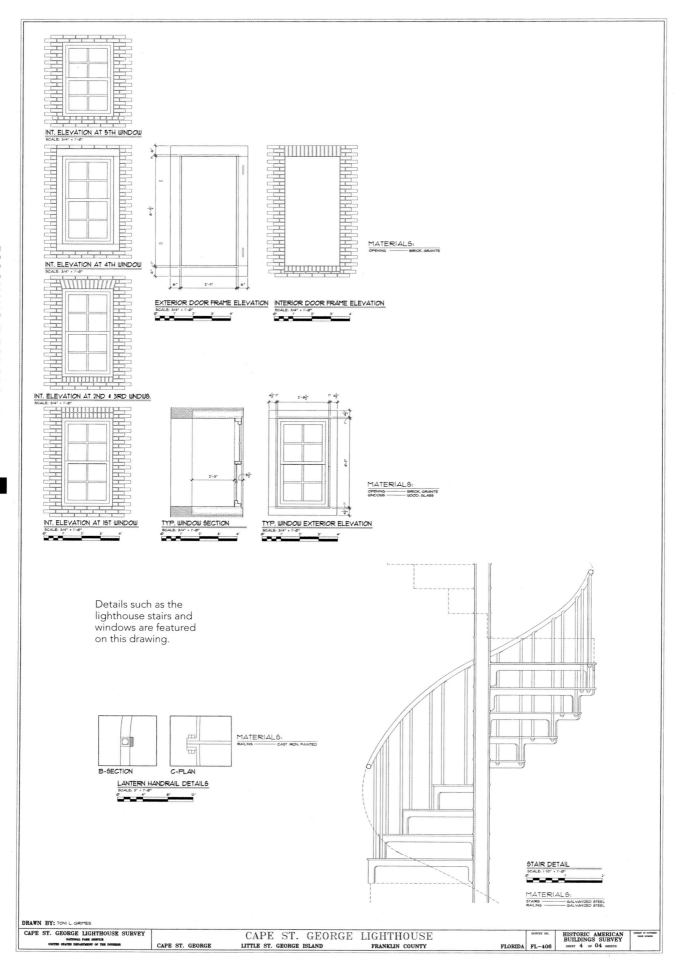

INT. ELEVATION AT 5TH WINDOW
SCALE: 3/4" = 1'-0"

INT. ELEVATION AT 4TH WINDOW
SCALE: 3/4" = 1'-0"

INT. ELEVATION AT 2ND & 3RD WNDWS.
SCALE: 3/4" = 1'-0"

INT. ELEVATION AT 1ST WINDOW
SCALE: 3/4" = 1'-0"

EXTERIOR DOOR FRAME ELEVATION
SCALE: 3/4" = 1'-0"

INTERIOR DOOR FRAME ELEVATION
SCALE: 3/4" = 1'-0"

MATERIALS:
OPENING ———— BRICK, GRANITE

TYP. WINDOW SECTION
SCALE: 3/4" = 1'-0"

TYP. WINDOW EXTERIOR ELEVATION
SCALE: 3/4" = 1'-0"

MATERIALS:
OPENING ———— BRICK, GRANITE
WINDOWS ———— WOOD, GLASS

Details such as the
lighthouse stairs and
windows are featured
on this drawing.

B-SECTION   C-PLAN
LANTERN HANDRAIL DETAILS
SCALE: 3" = 1'-0"

MATERIALS:
RAILING ———— CAST IRON, PAINTED

STAIR DETAIL
SCALE: 1 1/2" = 1'-0"

MATERIALS:
STAIRS ———— GALVANIZED STEEL
RAILING ———— GALVANIZED STEEL

DRAWN BY: TONI L. GRIMES
CAPE ST. GEORGE LIGHTHOUSE SURVEY
NATIONAL PARK SERVICE
UNITED STATES DEPARTMENT OF THE INTERIOR

CAPE ST. GEORGE LIGHTHOUSE
CAPE ST. GEORGE   LITTLE ST. GEORGE ISLAND   FRANKLIN COUNTY   FLORIDA | FL-406

SURVEY NO.
HISTORIC AMERICAN
BUILDINGS SURVEY
SHEET 4 OF 04 SHEETS

The leaning tower, shown here, remained standing until 2005, when it collapsed into the Gulf of Mexico.

37

CAPE SPENCER LIGHTHOUSE

GLACIER BAY NATIONAL PARK, ALASKA
BUILT IN 1925

One of the most remote lighthouse locations, Cape Spencer is a small island located near the entrance of the Icy Strait and Cross Sound. Keepers serving their year-long watch on the island had to endure incredibly harsh elements and were often forced to conserve their food, as the ships and helicopters bringing fresh supplies were usually delayed by inclement weather. The lighthouse is an extremely important navigational point for ships traveling around Alaska, marking the divide between the Inner and Outer Passages. Ships use the Cape Spencer Lighthouse as a guide to navigate into Cross Sound and the Icy Strait, a path that allows them to travel in the relatively calm waters of the Inner Passage rather than face the rough northern seas of the Outer Passage. Construction on this crucial lighthouse began in 1924 and was finished in 1925. Cape Spencer was lit by a third-order Fresnel lens, which was later removed in 1974. Although no longer manned, the Cape Spencer Lighthouse is still used by ships to mark the path to the Inner Passage.

The Cape Spencer Lighthouse is an important navigational point for sailors traveling around the coast of Alaska, helping them locate the calm waters of the Inner Passage.

The lighthouse is built on Cape Spencer, a small island situated at the entrance of Cross Sound and the Icy Straight.

40

The Cape Spencer Lighthouse helipad was built so helicopters could deliver supplies and transport work crews and keepers back and forth from the mainland.

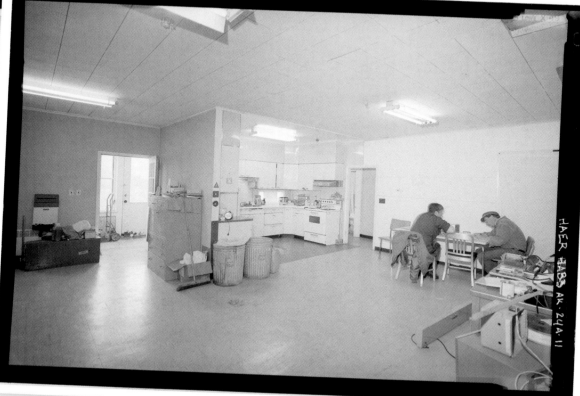

Due to the remote location of the lighthouse and the harsh weather and seas, keepers for the Cape Spencer Lighthouse served for only one year before being rotated to a new site.

Cape Spencer was lit by a third-order Fresnel lens until it was removed in 1974.

43

The light was placed in a tower that extended 25' above the lighthouse building.

The Cape Spencer Lighthouse, now cared for by the United States Coast Guard, is still used for navigation today.

Kraig Anderson

Kraig Anderson

Cedar Point Lighthouse

PLYMOUTH COUNTY, MASSACHUSETTS
BUILT IN 1811

Cedar Point, or Scituate, Lighthouse is the country's eleventh oldest lighthouse and was completed in 1811 to help guide commercial fishing vessels in and out of Scituate Harbor. Two daughters of the first lighthouse keeper are said to have frightened a British warship out of the harbor during the War of 1812 by playing military marches on a fife and drum. The original stone tower was 25' tall, but in 1827, a 15' brick extension was added, along with a new light. Several changes were made to the lighthouse during the mid-1800s. A red light was installed to shine out of the lighthouse's lower windows in order to prevent sailors from confusing it with the Boston light a few miles up the shore. In 1855, the lighthouse temporarily inherited a Fresnel lens from the nearby Minot's Ledge Lighthouse, which had collapsed. After the reconstruction of the Minot's Ledge tower, the lens was returned. In 1860, a breakwater was built in the harbor, and a light placed on a spar at the breakwater's edge replaced the Cedar Point light. The Cedar Point keeper's quarters were still occupied by individuals attending the new breakwater light. A family hired by the Scituate Historical Society now lives in and cares for the Cedar Point Lighthouse. The keeper's blog can be visited at *oldscituatelight.blogspot.com*.

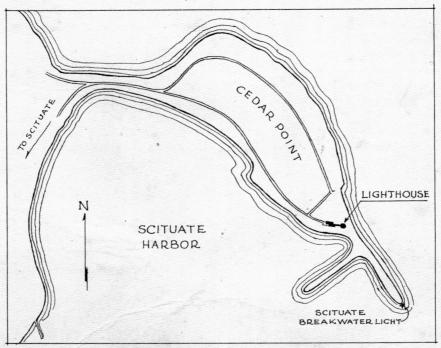

SKETCH MAP SHOWING LOCATION

HISTORIC AMERICAN BUILDINGS SURVEY
U.S. DEPARTMENT OF THE INTERIOR
NATIONAL PARK SERVICE
BRANCH OF PLANS AND DESIGN

MEASURED: MARCH 2-MARCH 24, 1934
DRAWN: MARCH 21-MARCH 30, 1934
MEASUREMENTS CHECKED: E.I.W. MARCH 31, 1934

DRAWINGS APPROVED: _____, DISTRICT OFFICER.
DRAWINGS APPROVED: _____, CHIEF ARCHITECT.
ACCEPTED FOR LIBRARY OF CONGRESS: _____

DISTRICT NO.2-MASSACHUSETTS
FRANK CHOUTEAU BROWN
DISTRICT OFFICER-16 BRIMMER ST.
BOSTON-MASSACHUSETTS
FIELD MEASUREMENTS BY
EDWIN I. WILSON
EGYPT-MASSACHUSETTS

SURVEY NO. 2-22
SHEETS 1-5

INDEX NO. MASS.
12-Scit. v
1-

Cedar Point, or Scituate, Lighthouse is the eleventh oldest lighthouse in the country.

This elevation shows the west side of the keeper's quarters, which were attached to the lighthouse tower.

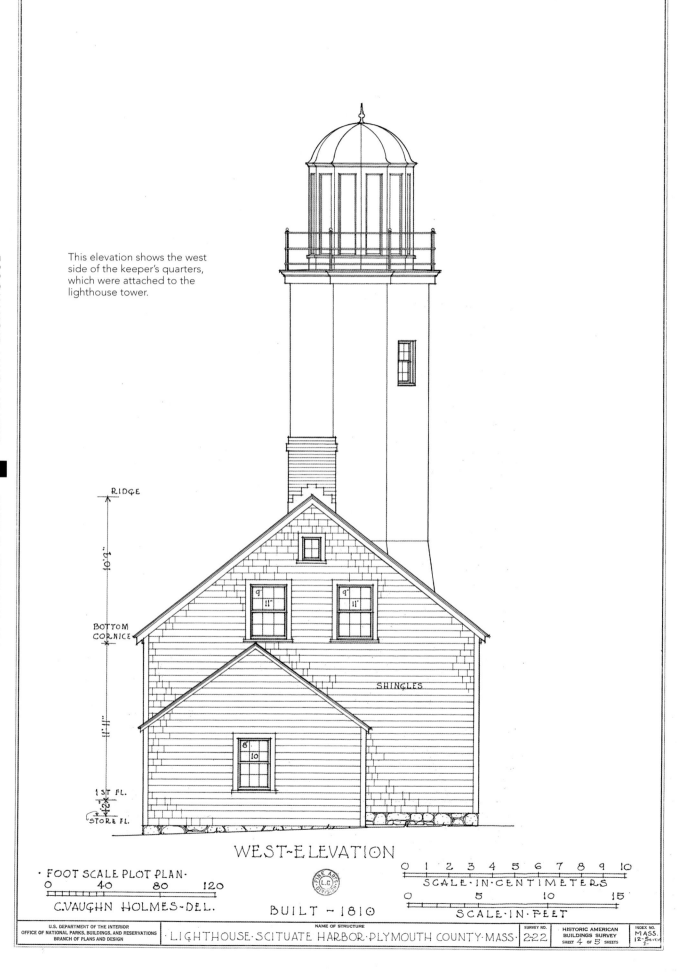

RIDGE

10'9"

BOTTOM CORNICE

11'11"

SHINGLES

9'
11"

9'
11"

8'
10"

1 ST FL.

STORE FL.

WEST·ELEVATION

· FOOT SCALE PLOT PLAN ·
0   40   80   120

C.VAUGHN HOLMES·DEL.

BUILT ~ 1810

0 1 2 3 4 5 6 7 8 9 10
SCALE·IN·CENTIMETERS

0   5   10   15
SCALE·IN·FEET

U.S. DEPARTMENT OF THE INTERIOR
OFFICE OF NATIONAL PARKS, BUILDINGS, AND RESERVATIONS
BRANCH OF PLANS AND DESIGN

NAME OF STRUCTURE
LIGHTHOUSE·SCITUATE HARBOR·PLYMOUTH COUNTY·MASS·

SURVEY NO.
2·22

HISTORIC AMERICAN
BUILDINGS SURVEY
SHEET 4 OF 5 SHEETS

INDEX NO.
MASS.
12-Scit.V

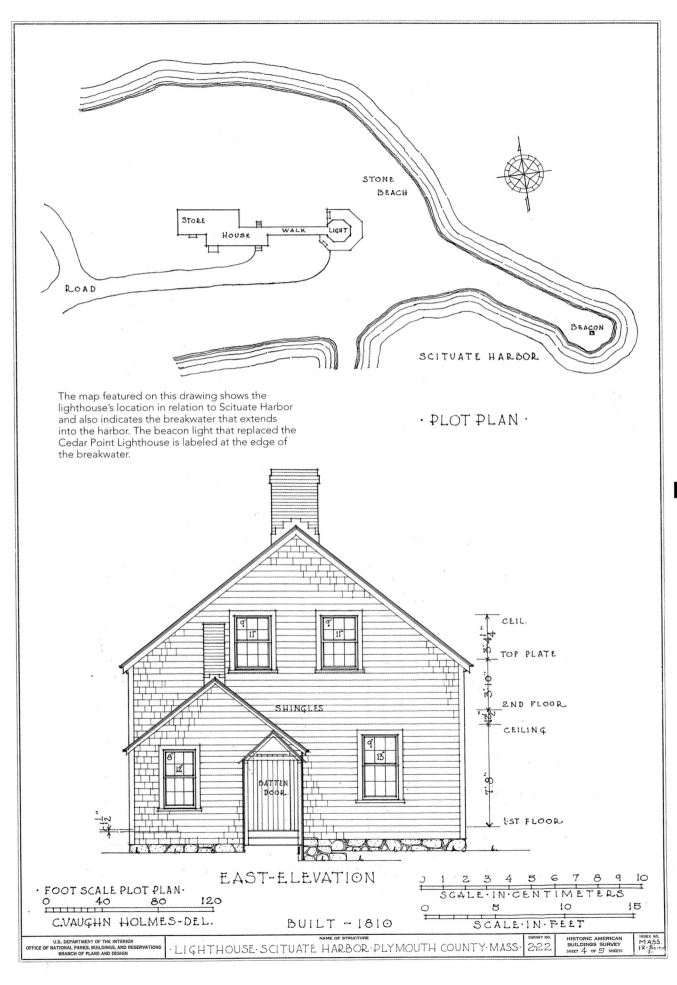

STONE
BEACH

STORE
HOUSE   WALK   LIGHT

ROAD

BEACON

SCITUATE HARBOR

The map featured on this drawing shows the
lighthouse's location in relation to Scituate Harbor
and also indicates the breakwater that extends
into the harbor. The beacon light that replaced the
Cedar Point Lighthouse is labeled at the edge of
the breakwater.

· PLOT PLAN ·

CEIL.

TOP PLATE

2ND FLOOR
CEILING

SHINGLES

BATTEN
DOOR.

1ST FLOOR

EAST · ELEVATION

· FOOT SCALE PLOT PLAN ·
0   40   80   120

C. VAUGHN HOLMES · DEL.

BUILT ~ 1810

0 1 2 3 4 5 6 7 8 9 10
SCALE · IN · CENTIMETERS

0   5   10   15
SCALE · IN · FEET

U.S. DEPARTMENT OF THE INTERIOR
OFFICE OF NATIONAL PARKS, BUILDINGS, AND RESERVATIONS
BRANCH OF PLANS AND DESIGN

NAME OF STRUCTURE
· LIGHTHOUSE · SCITUATE HARBOR · PLYMOUTH COUNTY · MASS ·

SURVEY NO.
2·22

HISTORIC AMERICAN
BUILDINGS SURVEY
SHEET 4 OF 5 SHEETS

INDEX NO.
MASS.
12-SCITY
1-

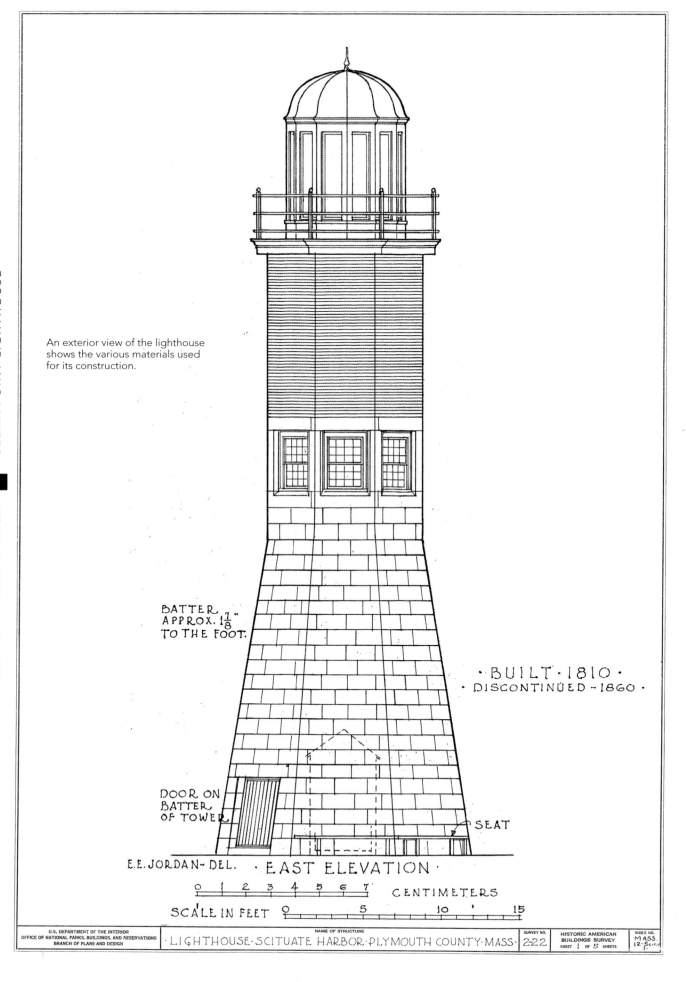

An exterior view of the lighthouse shows the various materials used for its construction.

BATTER
APPROX. $1\frac{7}{8}$"
TO THE FOOT.

·BUILT·1810·
·DISCONTINUED·1860·

DOOR ON
BATTER
OF TOWER

SEAT

E.E. JORDAN-DEL. · EAST ELEVATION ·

0 1 2 3 4 5 6 7 CENTIMETERS

SCALE IN FEET 0   5   10   15

U.S. DEPARTMENT OF THE INTERIOR
OFFICE OF NATIONAL PARKS, BUILDINGS, AND RESERVATIONS
BRANCH OF PLANS AND DESIGN

NAME OF STRUCTURE
LIGHTHOUSE·SCITUATE HARBOR·PLYMOUTH COUNTY·MASS·

SURVEY NO. 2·22

HISTORIC AMERICAN
BUILDINGS SURVEY
SHEET 1 OF 5 SHEETS

INDEX NO.
MASS.
12-Scit.v
1

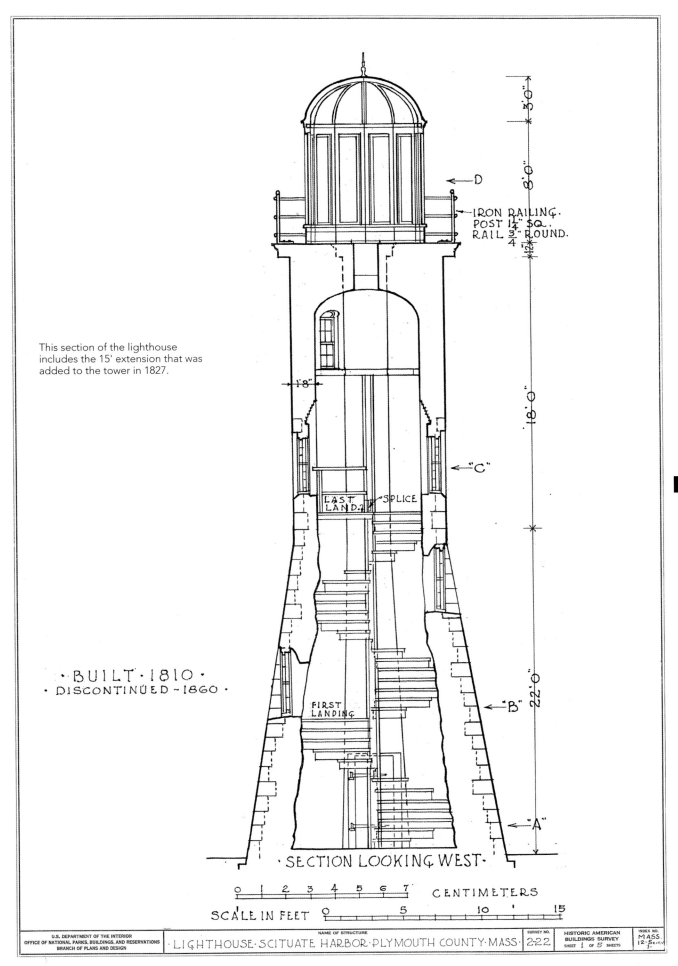

This section of the lighthouse includes the 15' extension that was added to the tower in 1827.

IRON RAILING.
POST 1¼" SQ.
RAIL ¾" ROUND.

1'8"

"C"

LAST LAND?   SPLICE

·BUILT·1810·
·DISCONTINUED~1860·

FIRST LANDING

"B"

"A"

·SECTION LOOKING WEST·

0 1 2 3 4 5 6 7   CENTIMETERS

SCALE IN FEET   0   5   10   15

U.S. DEPARTMENT OF THE INTERIOR
OFFICE OF NATIONAL PARKS, BUILDINGS, AND RESERVATIONS
BRANCH OF PLANS AND DESIGN

NAME OF STRUCTURE
LIGHTHOUSE·SCITUATE HARBOR·PLYMOUTH COUNTY·MASS·

SURVEY NO.
2-22

HISTORIC AMERICAN
BUILDINGS SURVEY
SHEET 1 OF 5 SHEETS

INDEX NO.
MASS.
12-SCIT.V

The interior of the keeper's quarters is shown here.

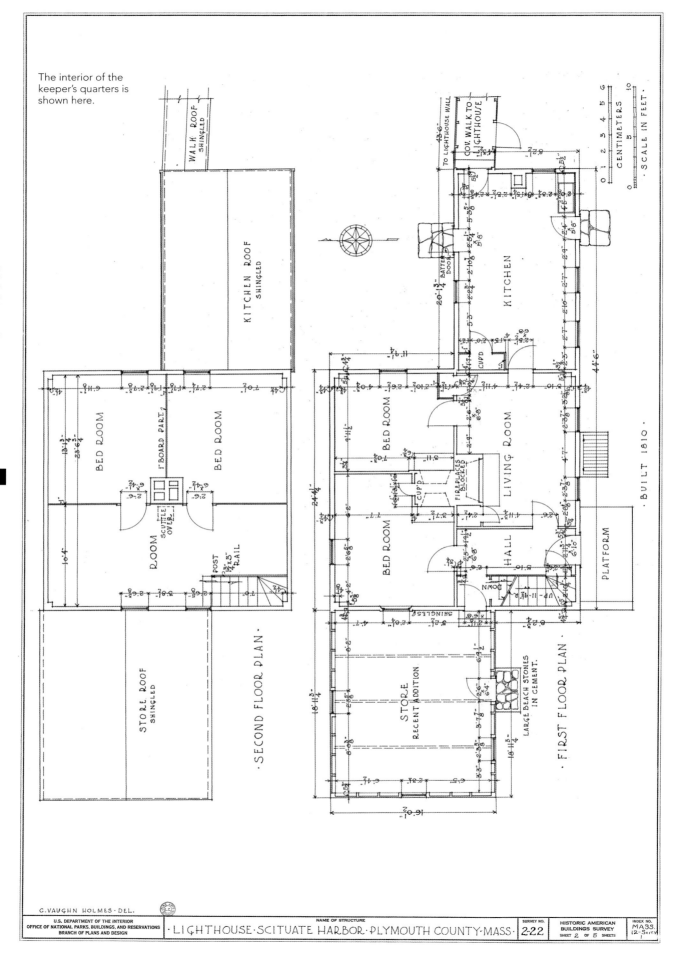

· SECOND FLOOR PLAN ·

· FIRST FLOOR PLAN ·

· BUILT 1810 ·

G. VAUGHN HOLMES · DEL.

U.S. DEPARTMENT OF THE INTERIOR
OFFICE OF NATIONAL PARKS, BUILDINGS, AND RESERVATIONS
BRANCH OF PLANS AND DESIGN

NAME OF STRUCTURE
· LIGHTHOUSE · SCITUATE HARBOR · PLYMOUTH COUNTY · MASS ·

SURVEY NO. 2·22

HISTORIC AMERICAN BUILDINGS SURVEY
SHEET 2 OF 5 SHEETS

INDEX NO. MASS. 12-SCITV

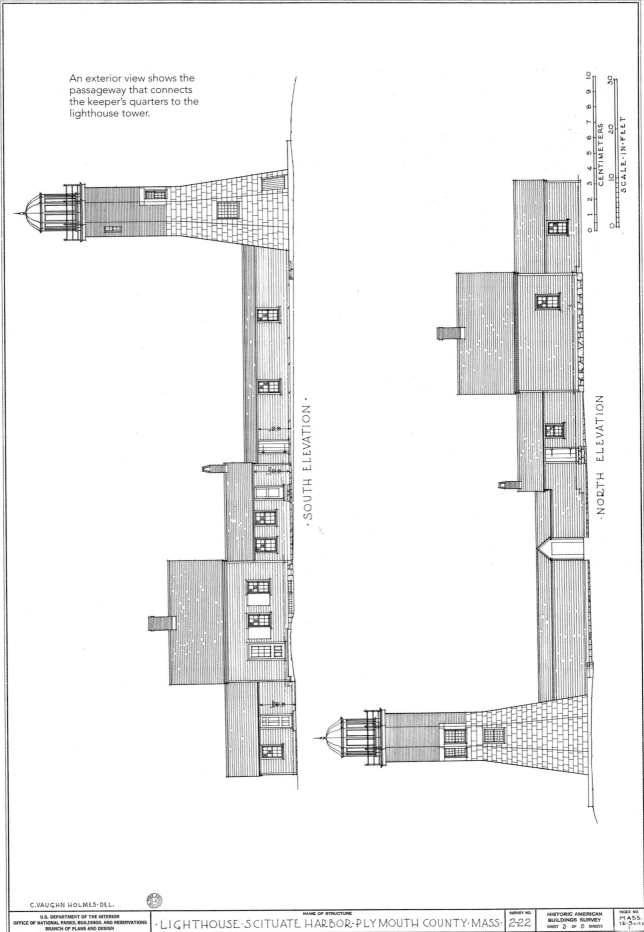

An exterior view shows the passageway that connects the keeper's quarters to the lighthouse tower.

· SOUTH ELEVATION ·

· NORTH ELEVATION ·

CENTIMETERS

SCALE · IN · FEET

C. VAUGHN HOLMES · DEL.

U.S. DEPARTMENT OF THE INTERIOR
OFFICE OF NATIONAL PARKS, BUILDINGS, AND RESERVATIONS
BRANCH OF PLANS AND DESIGN

NAME OF STRUCTURE
· LIGHTHOUSE · SCITUATE HARBOR · PLYMOUTH COUNTY · MASS ·

SURVEY NO.
2-22

HISTORIC AMERICAN
BUILDINGS SURVEY
SHEET 3 OF 5 SHEETS

INDEX NO.
MASS.
12-Scitu

Various details found throughout the Cedar Point Lighthouse, such as the windows and doors, are shown in this drawing.

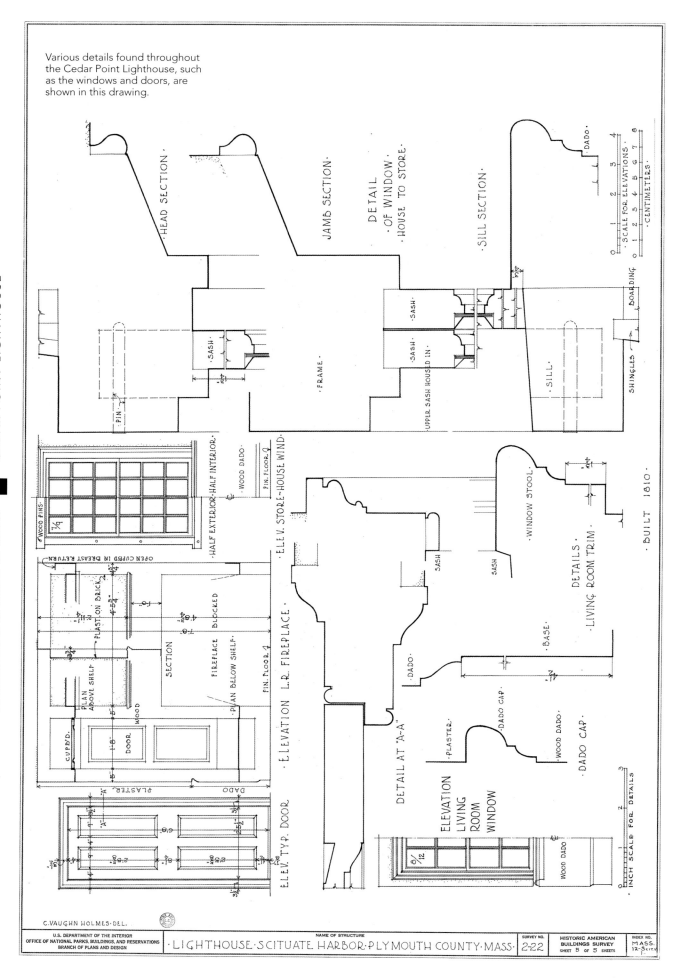

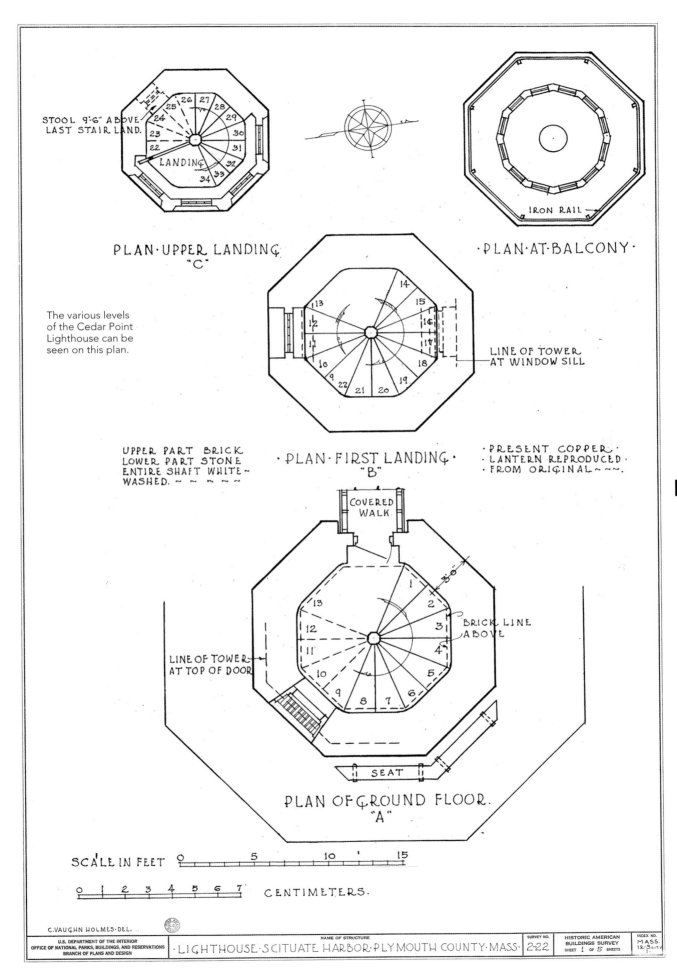

STOOL 9'-6" ABOVE
LAST STAIR LAND.

PLAN·UPPER LANDING
"C"

The various levels
of the Cedar Point
Lighthouse can be
seen on this plan.

PLAN·AT·BALCONY·

IRON RAIL

LINE OF TOWER
AT WINDOW SILL

·PLAN·FIRST LANDING·
"B"

UPPER PART BRICK
LOWER PART STONE
ENTIRE SHAFT WHITE-
WASHED. ~ ~ ~ ~

·PRESENT COPPER·
·LANTERN REPRODUCED·
·FROM ORIGINAL·~~.

COVERED
WALK

BRICK LINE
ABOVE

LINE OF TOWER
AT TOP OF DOOR

SEAT

PLAN OF GROUND FLOOR.
"A"

SCALE IN FEET 0 5 10 15

0 1 2 3 4 5 6 7 CENTIMETERS.

C. VAUGHN HOLMES·DEL.

U.S. DEPARTMENT OF THE INTERIOR
OFFICE OF NATIONAL PARKS, BUILDINGS, AND RESERVATIONS
BRANCH OF PLANS AND DESIGN

NAME OF STRUCTURE
·LIGHTHOUSE·SCITUATE HARBOR·PLYMOUTH COUNTY·MASS·

SURVEY NO.
2-22

HISTORIC AMERICAN
BUILDINGS SURVEY
SHEET 1 OF 5 SHEETS

INDEX NO.
MASS.
12-Scit.y

In 1860, the original lighthouse, pictured here, was replaced by a light located at the end of a newly built breakwater that extended into Scituate Harbor.

Kraig Anderson

Keepers tending the new beacon continued to live in the Cedar Point keeper's quarters until the early 1920s, when an automated light was installed.

A family hired by the Scituate Historical Society currently resides in and cares for the lighthouse.

HEREFORD INLET LIGHT STATION

CAPE MAY COUNTY, NEW JERSEY
BUILT IN 1874

Hereford Inlet provides a passageway from the Atlantic Ocean to the Intracoastal Waterway, which leads from Maine to Florida. The inlet was originally used by whalers and would later become a high traffic area as shipping increased on the East Coast. The entrance to the inlet is a danger zone, filled with strong currents and sandbars that often shift over time. Groundings and shipwrecks were a common occurrence, leading the United States Lighthouse Board to propose the building of a small lighthouse to mark the entrance to the inlet in 1871. Hereford Inlet Light Station was completed in 1874 and fitted with a fourth-order Fresnel lens. The station is a wonderful representation of Swiss Carpenter Gothic or Stick Style architecture. A boat-house, oil house, barn, privy, storehouse, and lifesaving station No. 36 were also built around the lighthouse. After suffering storm damage, the lighthouse was moved 150' in 1913. The original light was replaced with an automated one in 1964.

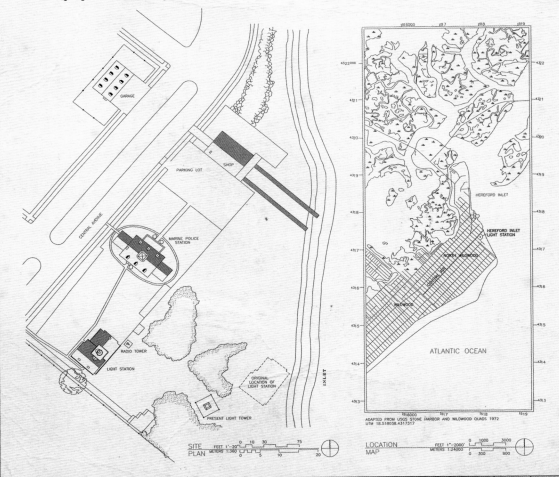

SITE PLAN — FEET 1"=20' METERS 1:360

LOCATION MAP — FEET 1"=2000' METERS 1:24000

ADAPTED FROM USGS STONE HARBOR AND WILDWOOD QUADS 1972
UTM 18.518038.4317317

FRANCIS G. VITETTA ASSOCIATES
OFFICE OF ARCHAEOLOGY AND HISTORIC PRESERVATION
HERITAGE CONSERVATION AND RECREATION SERVICE
UNITED STATES DEPARTMENT OF THE INTERIOR

NAME AND LOCATION OF STRUCTURE
HEREFORD INLET LIGHT STATION
CENTRAL AVE. AT CHESTNUT STREET   NORTH WILDWOOD   CAPE MAY COUNTY   NEW JERSEY

SURVEY NO.
NJ1238

HISTORIC AMERICAN BUILDINGS SURVEY
SHEET 1 OF 7 SHEETS
LIBRARY OF CONGRESS INDEX NUMBER

The Hereford Inlet Light Station was used to guide ships through Hereford Inlet to the Intracoastal Waterway.

The Hereford Lighthouse and gardens are maintained to preserve the past for all of us. The following rules must be observed.

Kraig Anderson

The basement and the first
floor of the lighthouse are
featured on this plan.

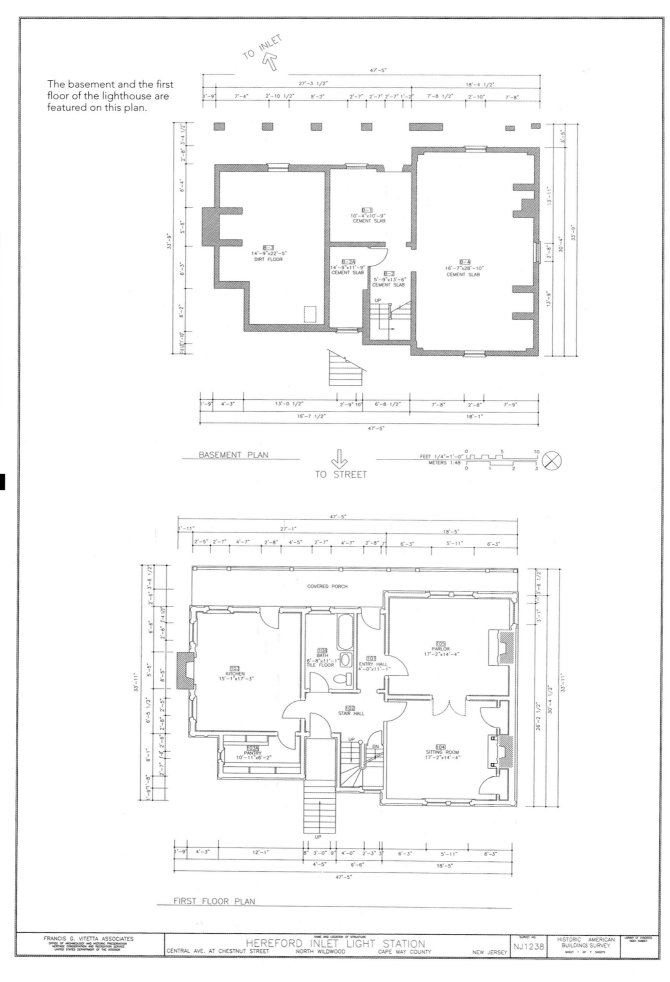

BASEMENT PLAN

TO STREET

FIRST FLOOR PLAN

FRANCIS G. VITETTA ASSOCIATES
OFFICE OF ARCHAEOLOGY AND HISTORIC PRESERVATION
HERITAGE CONSERVATION AND RECREATION SERVICE
UNITED STATES DEPARTMENT OF THE INTERIOR

HEREFORD INLET LIGHT STATION
CENTRAL AVE. AT CHESTNUT STREET   NORTH WILDWOOD   CAPE MAY COUNTY   NEW JERSEY

NJ1238

HISTORIC AMERICAN
BUILDINGS SURVEY
SHEET 1 OF 7 SHEETS

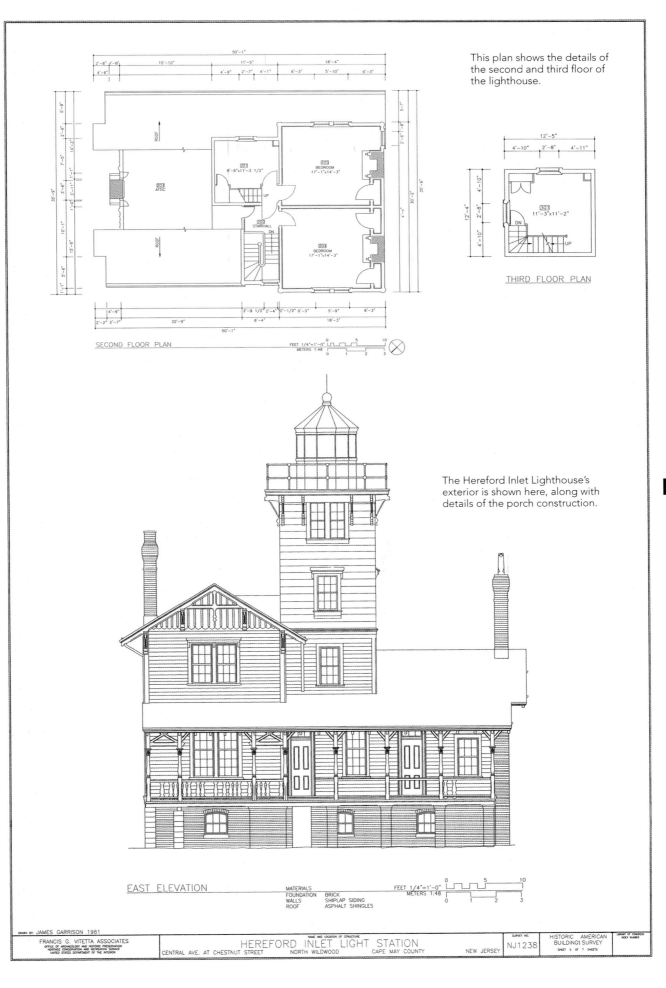

This plan shows the details of the second and third floor of the lighthouse.

THIRD FLOOR PLAN

SECOND FLOOR PLAN

FEET 1/4"=1'-0"
METERS 1:48

The Hereford Inlet Lighthouse's exterior is shown here, along with details of the porch construction.

EAST ELEVATION

MATERIALS
FOUNDATION   BRICK
WALLS   SHIPLAP SIDING
ROOF   ASPHALT SHINGLES

FEET 1/4"=1'-0"
METERS 1:48

DRAWN BY: JAMES GARRISON 1981

FRANCIS G. VITETTA ASSOCIATES
OFFICE OF ARCHAEOLOGY AND HISTORIC PRESERVATION
HERITAGE CONSERVATION AND RECREATION SERVICE
UNITED STATES DEPARTMENT OF THE INTERIOR

NAME AND LOCATION OF STRUCTURE
HEREFORD INLET LIGHT STATION
CENTRAL AVE. AT CHESTNUT STREET   NORTH WILDWOOD   CAPE MAY COUNTY   NEW JERSEY

SURVEY NO.
NJ1238

HISTORIC AMERICAN
BUILDINGS SURVEY
SHEET 5 OF 7 SHEETS

LIBRARY OF CONGRESS
INDEX NUMBER

A section of the lighthouse shows
how it was constructed.

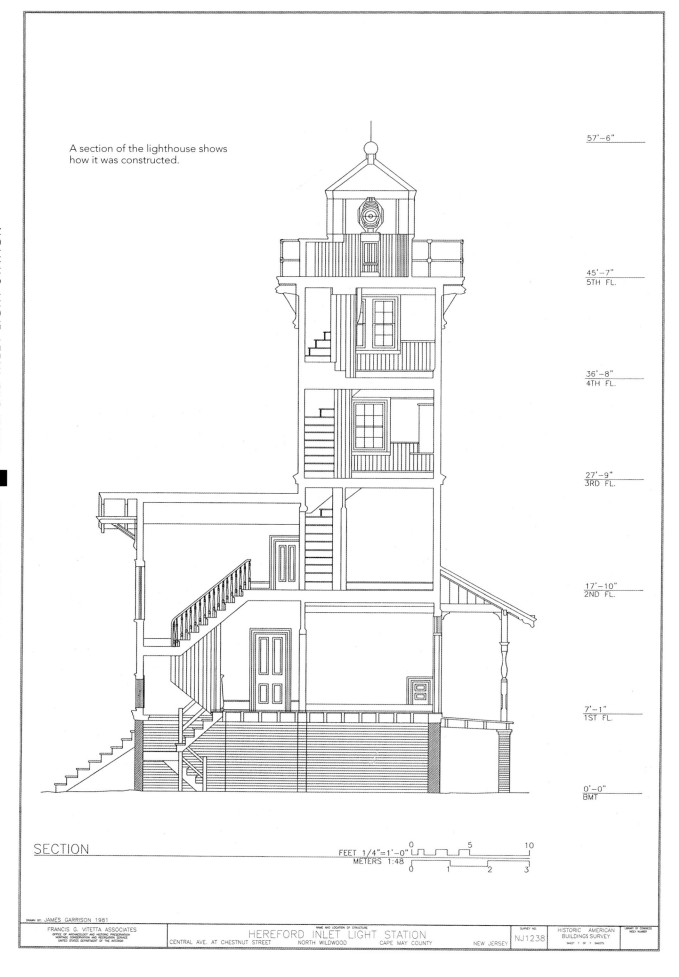

57'–6"

45'–7"
5TH FL.

36'–8"
4TH FL.

27'–9"
3RD FL.

17'–10"
2ND FL.

7'–1"
1ST FL.

0'–0"
BMT

SECTION

FEET 1/4"=1'–0"   0   5   10
METERS 1:48   0   1   2   3

DRAWN BY: JAMES GARRISON 1981

FRANCIS G. VITETTA ASSOCIATES
OFFICE OF ARCHAEOLOGY AND HISTORIC PRESERVATION
HERITAGE CONSERVATION AND RECREATION SERVICE
UNITED STATES DEPARTMENT OF THE INTERIOR

NAME AND LOCATION OF STRUCTURE
HEREFORD INLET LIGHT STATION
CENTRAL AVE. AT CHESTNUT STREET   NORTH WILDWOOD   CAPE MAY COUNTY   NEW JERSEY

SURVEY NO.
NJ1238

HISTORIC AMERICAN
BUILDINGS SURVEY
SHEET 7 OF 7 SHEETS

LIBRARY OF CONGRESS
INDEX NUMBER

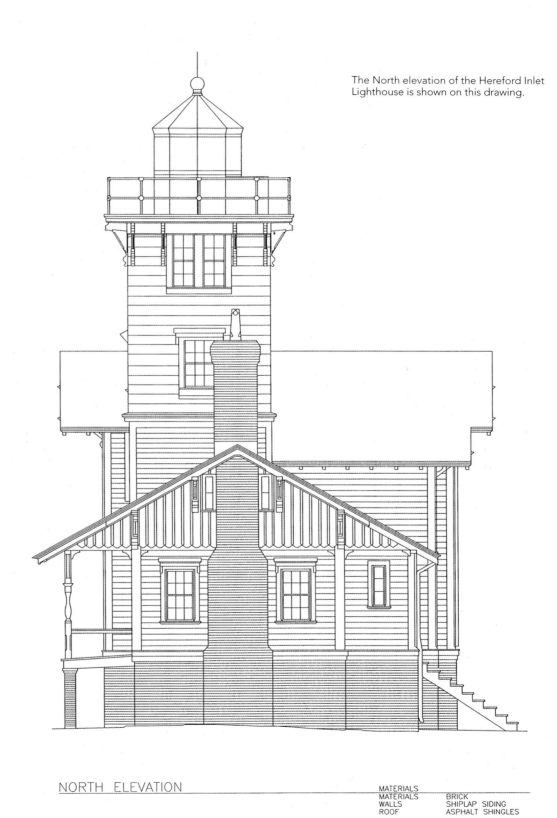

The North elevation of the Hereford Inlet Lighthouse is shown on this drawing.

NORTH ELEVATION

MATERIALS	
MATERIALS	BRICK
WALLS	SHIPLAP SIDING
ROOF	ASPHALT SHINGLES

DRAWN BY: JAMES GARRISON 1981

FRANCIS G. VITETTA ASSOCIATES
OFFICE OF ARCHAEOLOGY AND HISTORIC PRESERVATION
HERITAGE CONSERVATION AND RECREATION SERVICE
UNITED STATES DEPARTMENT OF THE INTERIOR

NAME AND LOCATION OF STRUCTURE
HEREFORD INLET LIGHT STATION
CENTRAL AVE. AT CHESTNUT STREET   NORTH WILDWOOD   CAPE MAY COUNTY   NEW JERSEY

SURVEY NO.
NJ1238

HISTORIC AMERICAN
BUILDINGS SURVEY
SHEET 6 OF 7 SHEETS

LIBRARY OF CONGRESS
INDEX NUMBER

The tower that housed Hereford Inlet's
fourth-order Fresnel lens can be seen here.

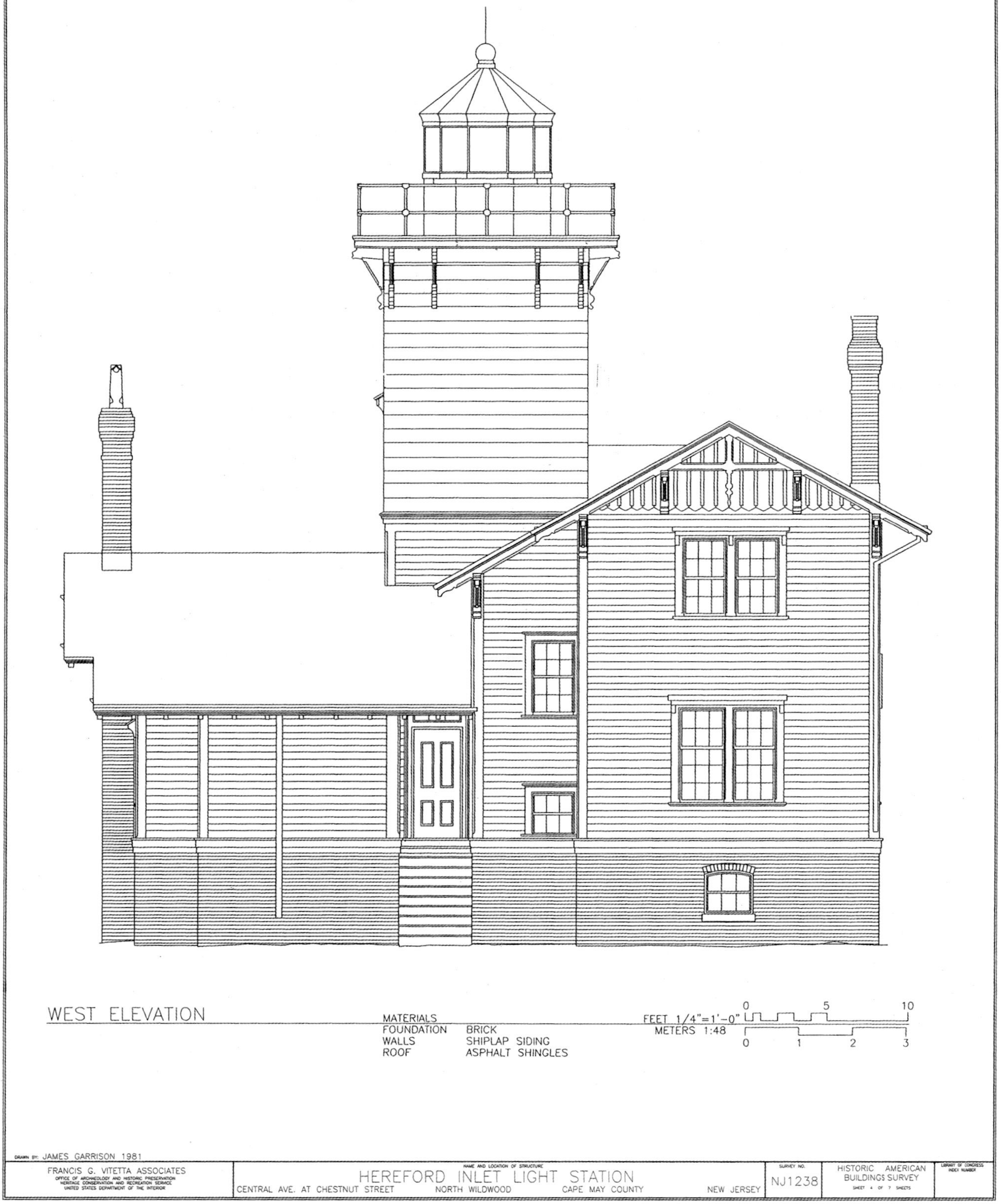

WEST ELEVATION

MATERIALS
FOUNDATION   BRICK
WALLS   SHIPLAP SIDING
ROOF   ASPHALT SHINGLES

FEET 1/4"=1'-0"
METERS 1:48

0   5   10

0   1   2   3

DRAWN BY: JAMES GARRISON 1981

FRANCIS G. VITETTA ASSOCIATES
OFFICE OF ARCHAEOLOGY AND HISTORIC PRESERVATION
HERITAGE CONSERVATION AND RECREATION SERVICE
UNITED STATES DEPARTMENT OF THE INTERIOR

NAME AND LOCATION OF STRUCTURE
HEREFORD INLET LIGHT STATION
CENTRAL AVE. AT CHESTNUT STREET   NORTH WILDWOOD   CAPE MAY COUNTY   NEW JERSEY

SURVEY NO.
NJ1238

HISTORIC AMERICAN
BUILDINGS SURVEY
SHEET 4 OF 7 SHEETS

LIBRARY OF CONGRESS
INDEX NUMBER

The lighthouse was moved 150' in 1913 after a severe storm caused the ocean to swell, bringing it, literally, to the front door of the lighthouse.

Kraig Anderson

Jones Point Lighthouse

Alexandria vicinity, Virginia
Built in 1855

The Jones Point Lighthouse, built in 1855, was used to help ships bound for Alexandria navigate around the sandbars of the Potomac River. The lighthouse is a small two-story rectangular structure measuring 19' by 38'. A retaining wall was built around the building in 1861 to keep it safe from flooding. The light was used by ships on the river until 1926 when it was replaced by another nearby light tower. After the lighthouse was deactivated, it was given to the Mount Vernon Chapter of the Daughters of the American Revolution (DAR). During World War II, however, the DAR was denied access to the light because it was located on land that was commandeered by the Army for use by the Signal Corps. For years the lighthouse was left unattended, and it fell into disrepair. Although the lighthouse was given to the National Park Service in 1964, the DAR maintained its efforts to care for it, and the lighthouse was eventually restored.

66

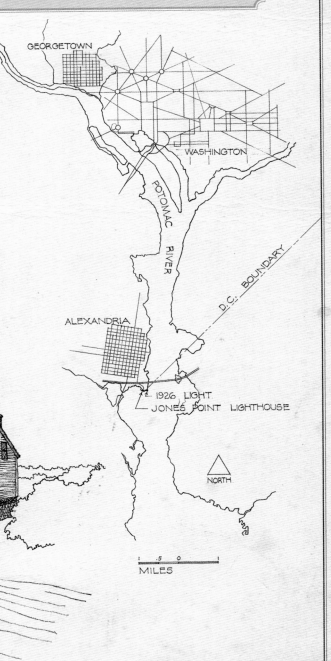

SUMMER STUDENT TEAM FOR N.C.D.C. WASHINGTON, D.C. 1965
UNDER DIRECTION OF UNITED STATES DEPARTMENT OF THE INTERIOR NATIONAL PARK SERVICE, BRANCH OF PLANS AND DESIGN

NAME OF STRUCTURE
JONES POINT LIGHTHOUSE
JONES POINT, ALEXANDRIA, VIRGINIA

SURVEY NO.
VA-641

HISTORIC AMERICAN BUILDINGS SURVEY
SHEET 1 OF 6 SHEETS

The Jones Point Lighthouse
is located on the bank of the
Potomac and was used to guide
ships on the river.

The lighthouse contained a fifth-order Fresnel lens. Although a fifth-order lens is the second smallest Fresnel lens, the Jones Point light could be seen from 9 miles away.

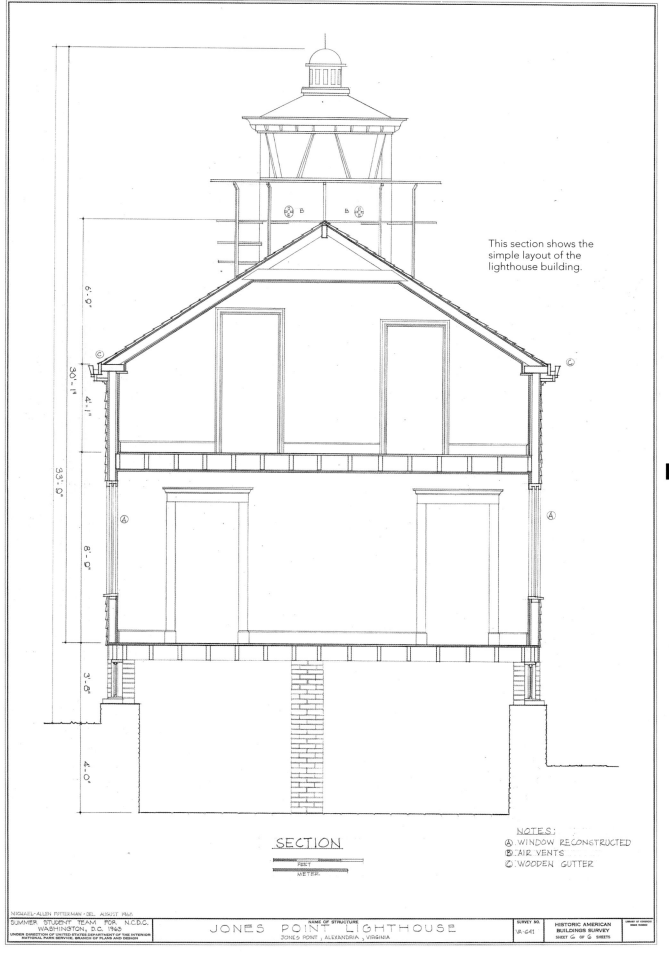

This section shows the simple layout of the lighthouse building.

6'-9"

30'-1"

4'-1"

33'-0"

8'-0"

3'-8"

4'-0"

SECTION

FEET

METER

NOTES:
Ⓐ WINDOW RECONSTRUCTED
Ⓑ AIR VENTS
Ⓒ WOODEN GUTTER

MICHAEL-ALLEN FUTTERMAN · DEL. AUGUST 1963

SUMMER STUDENT TEAM FOR N.C.D.C.
WASHINGTON, D.C. 1963
UNDER DIRECTION OF UNITED STATES DEPARTMENT OF THE INTERIOR
NATIONAL PARK SERVICE, BRANCH OF PLANS AND DESIGN

NAME OF STRUCTURE

JONES POINT LIGHTHOUSE
JONES POINT, ALEXANDRIA, VIRGINIA

SURVEY NO.
VA-641

HISTORIC AMERICAN
BUILDINGS SURVEY
SHEET 6 OF 6 SHEETS

LIBRARY OF CONGRESS
INDEX NUMBER

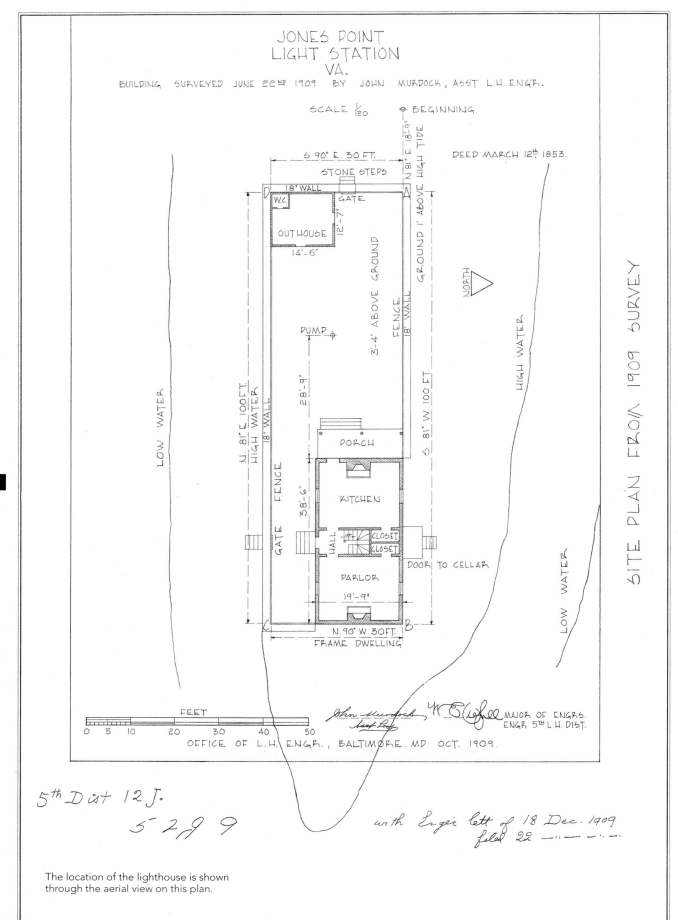

The location of the lighthouse is shown through the aerial view on this plan.

This exterior view shows where
the Fresnel lens was located on
the lighthouse roof.

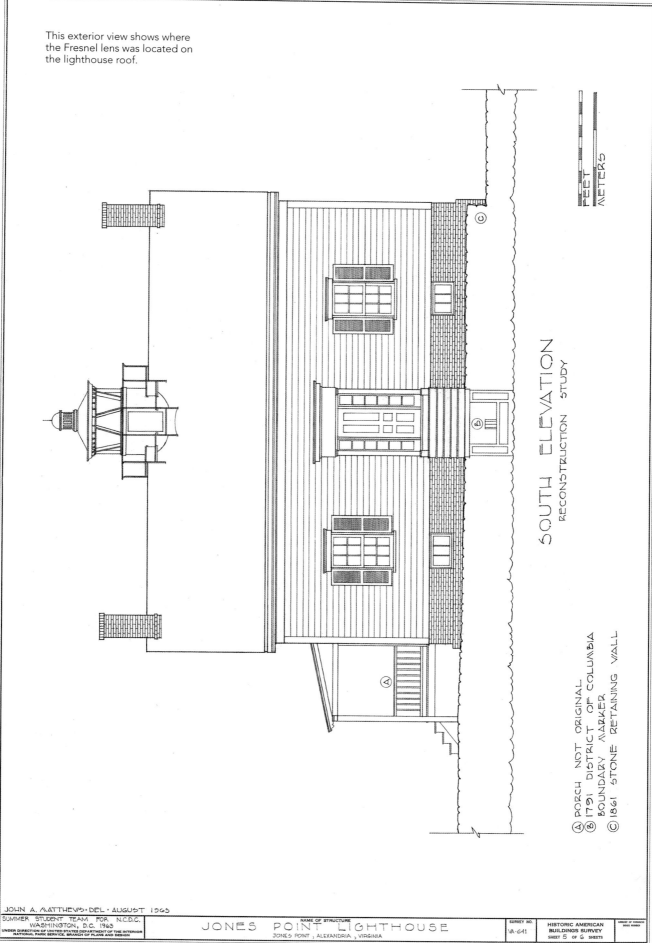

SOUTH ELEVATION

RECONSTRUCTION STUDY

Ⓐ PORCH NOT ORIGINAL
Ⓑ 1791 DISTRICT OF COLUMBIA
    BOUNDARY MARKER
Ⓒ 1861 STONE RETAINING WALL

FEET
METERS

JOHN A. MATTHEWS·DEL·AUGUST 1963

SUMMER STUDENT TEAM FOR N.C.D.C.
WASHINGTON, D.C. 1963
UNDER DIRECTION OF UNITED STATES DEPARTMENT OF THE INTERIOR
NATIONAL PARK SERVICE, BRANCH OF PLANS AND DESIGN

NAME OF STRUCTURE
JONES POINT LIGHTHOUSE
JONES POINT, ALEXANDRIA, VIRGINIA

SURVEY NO.
VA·641

HISTORIC AMERICAN
BUILDINGS SURVEY
SHEET 5 OF 6 SHEETS

LIGHTHOUSES: A CLOSE-UP LOOK

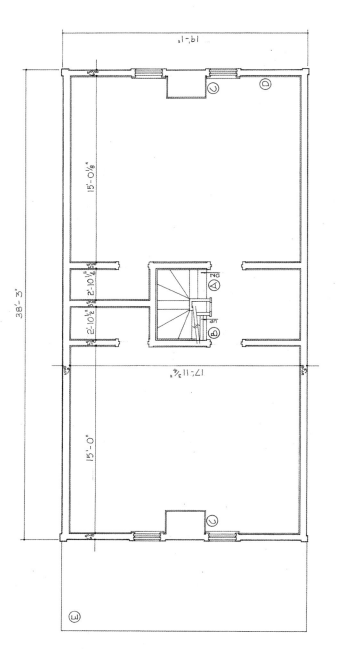

SECOND FLOOR PLAN

Ⓐ. STAIRWAY RECONSTRUCTED.

Ⓑ. SHIPS LADDER TO LANTERN HATCH ABOVE.

Ⓒ. LOCATION OF FORMER CHIMNEY.

Ⓓ. WALL MISSING.

Ⓔ. ROOF OF PORCH.

The lighthouse's first and second floors are shown on these plans along with notes detailing the changes made to the structure over the years.

JOHN C. WHITMIRE, DEL. AUG. 1963.

SUMMER STUDENT TEAM FOR N.C.D.C.
WASHINGTON D.C. 1963.
UNDER DIRECTION OF UNITED STATES DEPARTMENT OF THE INTERIOR
NATIONAL PARK SERVICE, BRANCH OF PLANS AND DESIGN

NAME OF STRUCTURE

JONES POINT LIGHTHOUSE.
JONES POINT, ALEXANDRIA, VIRGINIA

SURVEY NO.
VA-641

HISTORIC AMERICAN
BUILDINGS SURVEY
SHEET 4 OF 6 SHEETS

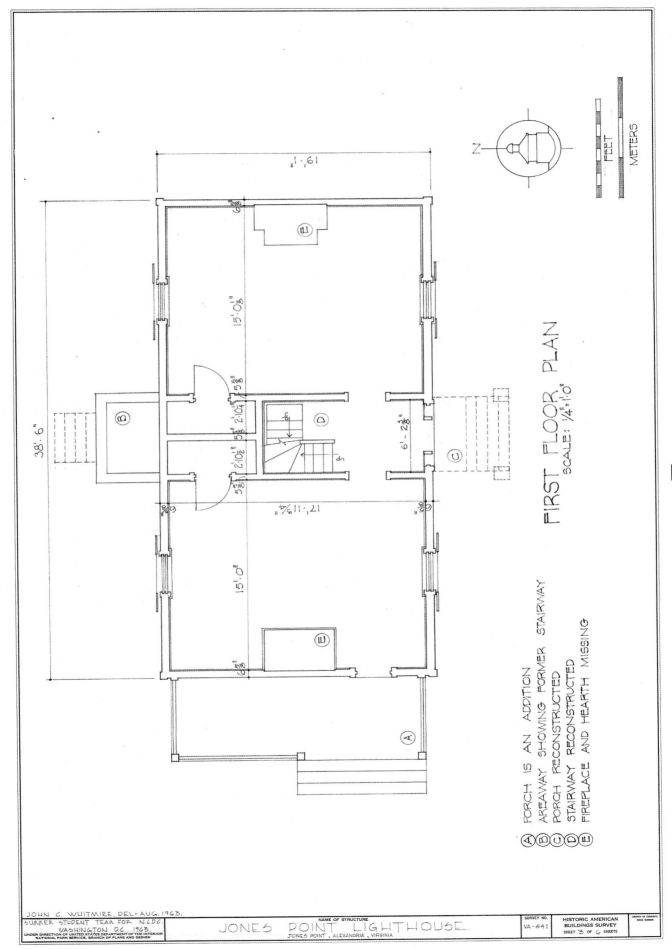

FIRST FLOOR PLAN
SCALE: ¼"=1'-0"

19'-1"

38'-6"

15'-0⅛"

5⅝"

2'-10¼"

2'-10½" 5⅝"

6'-2⅜"

17'-11¾"

15'-0"

6⅜"

6⅝"

dn

B

D

C

A

E

E

A PORCH IS AN ADDITION
B AREAWAY SHOWING FORMER STAIRWAY
C PORCH RECONSTRUCTED
D STAIRWAY RECONSTRUCTED
E FIREPLACE AND HEARTH MISSING

A B C D E

N

FEET

METERS

JOHN C. WHITMIRE, DEL. AUG. 1963.

SUMMER STUDENT TEAM FOR N.C.D.C.
WASHINGTON D.C., 1963.
UNDER DIRECTION OF UNITED STATES DEPARTMENT OF THE INTERIOR
NATIONAL PARK SERVICE, BRANCH OF PLANS AND DESIGN

NAME OF STRUCTURE
JONES POINT LIGHTHOUSE.
JONES POINT, ALEXANDRIA, VIRGINIA

SURVEY NO.
VA-641

HISTORIC AMERICAN
BUILDINGS SURVEY
SHEET 3 OF 6 SHEETS

LIBRARY OF CONGRESS
INDEX NUMBER

During World War II, the Army Signal Corps commandeered the land surrounding the Jones Point Lighthouse, and the structure fell into disrepair.

Kraig Anderson

Due to the efforts of the Mount Vernon Chapter of the Daughters of the American revolution, the lighthouse was restored in the years following WWII.

Kraig Anderson

Moloka'i (Kalaupapa) Light Station

Kalaupapa National Historic Park, Hawaii
Built in 1908

Most vessels traveling to the Hawaiian Islands in the 1800s passed through a channel of water between the islands of Moloka'i and Oahu, but, as a report made to Congress in the early 1900s explained, there was not a lighthouse on either island to help guide the ships. Although the necessity of a lighthouse was clear, and the Kalaupapa Peninsula on Moloka'i was the ideal location on which to build one, many people did not want the light constructed on the peninsula. As early as 1866, Kalaupapa had been used as a leper colony. It was feared that building a lighthouse near the colony would be unsafe for the construction workers, as well as future keepers and visitors. These concerns delayed the construction of a permanent light until 1908. The result was a 132' tower lit with a second-order Fresnel lens that would remain in place until the 1980s. All keepers, their families, and lighthouse visitors were required to use special passes to come and go from the peninsula in accordance with rules set by the Board of Health.

The Moloka'i Lighthouse was erected on the Kalaupapa Peninsula to guide ships through the waterway that passed between the islands of Moloka'i and Oahu.

HABS NO. HI-99-A-5

Construction on the Moloka'i Lighthouse did not begin until 1908
because the Kalaupapa Peninsula is also the location of a leper colony,
and many were hesitant to build a tower nearby.

The Moloka'i Lighthouse stands 132' tall and was lit by a second-order Fresnel lens until the 1980s.

Kraig Anderson

OUTER ISLAND LIGHT STATION

ASHLAND COUNTY, WISCONSIN
BUILT IN 1874

The Outer Island Light Station was built in 1874 to guide ships traveling to the ports of Duluth and Superior around the Apostle Islands, a group of small islands that extend into Lake Superior. The light was built on the outermost point of the islands, allowing ships to give the dangerous location a wide berth. The lighthouse stands about 90' tall and is made of brick. An enclosed passageway was built between the keeper's quarters and the lighthouse to provide shelter for the keeper during inclement weather. Until it was replaced by an automated light in 1961, the lighthouse used a third-order Fresnel lens that was turned by a weight-powered machine. A fog signal building was added to the lighthouse site in 1875, followed by a tramway that allowed keepers to easily transport supplies from the lighthouse to the newly constructed building. Today the Outer Island Light Station uses solar power to shine across Lake Superior.

80

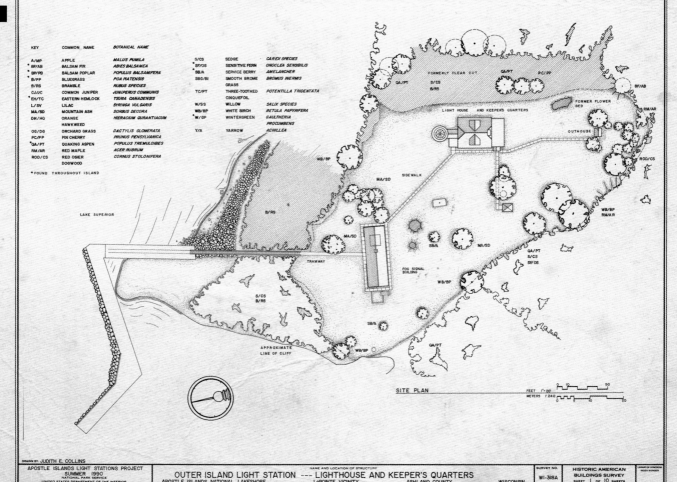

KEY	COMMON NAME	BOTANICAL NAME
A/MP	APPLE	MALUS PUMILA
* BF/AB	BALSAM FIR	ABIES BALSAMEA
*BP/PB	BALSAM POPLAR	POPULUS BALSAMIFERA
B/PP	BLUEGRASS	POA PRATENSIS
B/RS	BRAMBLE	RUBUS SPECIES
CJ/JC	COMMON JUNIPER	JUNIPERUS COMMUNIS
*EH/TC	EASTERN HEMLOCK	TSUGA CANADENSIS
L/SV	LILAC	SYRINGA VULGARIS
MA/SD	MOUNTAIN ASH	SORBUS DECORA
OH/HQ	ORANGE HAWKWEED	HERACIUM QUARANTIACUM
OG/DG	ORCHARD GRASS	DACTYLIS GLOMERATA
PC/PP	PIN CHERRY	PRUNUS PENSYLVANICA
*QA/PT	QUAKING ASPEN	POPULUS TREMULOIDES
RM/AR	RED MAPLE	ACER RUBRUM
ROD/CS	RED OSIER DOGWOOD	CORNUS STOLONIFERA

S/CS	SEDGE	CAREX SPECIES
* SF/OS	SENSITIVE FERN	ONOCLEA SENSIBILIS
SB/A	SERVICE BERRY	AMELANCHER
SBG/BI	SMOOTH BROME GRASS	BROMUS INERMS
TC/PT	THREE-TOOTHED CINQUEFOIL	POTENTILLA TRIDENTATA
W/SS	WILLOW	SALIX SPECIES
WB/BP	WHITE BIRCH	BETULA PAPYRIFERA
*W/GP	WINTERGREEN	GAULTHERIA PROCUMBENS
Y/A	YARROW	ACHILLEA

*FOUND THROUGHOUT ISLAND

LAKE SUPERIOR

SITE PLAN

FEET 1"=20'
METERS 1":240

DRAWN BY: JUDITH E. COLLINS

APOSTLE ISLANDS LIGHT STATIONS PROJECT
SUMMER 1990
NATIONAL PARK SERVICE
UNITED STATES DEPARTMENT OF THE INTERIOR

NAME AND LOCATION OF STRUCTURE
OUTER ISLAND LIGHT STATION --- LIGHTHOUSE AND KEEPER'S QUARTERS
APOSTLE ISLANDS NATIONAL LAKESHORE   LaPOINTE VICINITY   ASHLAND COUNTY   WISCONSIN

SURVEY NO.
WI-318A

HISTORIC AMERICAN BUILDINGS SURVEY
SHEET 1 OF 10 SHEETS

The Outer Island Light Station was built to guide ships around the Apostle Islands in Lake Superior.

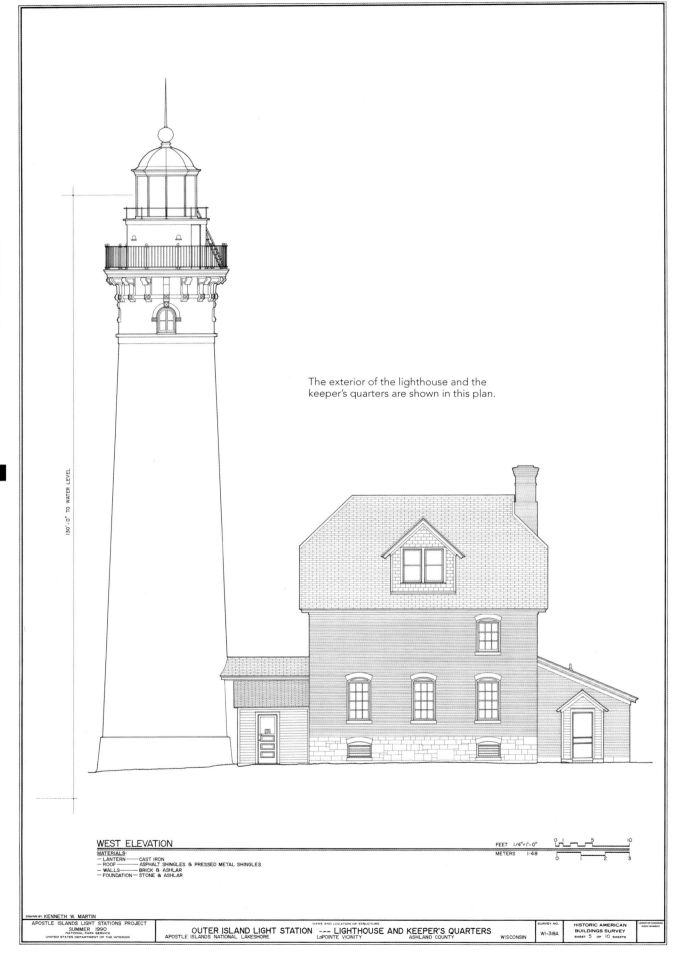

The exterior of the lighthouse and the keeper's quarters are shown in this plan.

130'-0" TO WATER LEVEL

WEST ELEVATION

MATERIALS:
— LANTERN —— CAST IRON
— ROOF ——— ASPHALT SHINGLES & PRESSED METAL SHINGLES
— WALLS ——— BRICK & ASHLAR
— FOUNDATION —STONE & ASHLAR

FEET 1/4"=1'-0"
METERS 1:48

0   5   10

0   1   2   3

DRAWN BY KENNETH W. MARTIN

APOSTLE ISLANDS LIGHT STATIONS PROJECT
SUMMER 1990
NATIONAL PARK SERVICE
UNITED STATES DEPARTMENT OF THE INTERIOR

NAME AND LOCATION OF STRUCTURE
OUTER ISLAND LIGHT STATION --- LIGHTHOUSE AND KEEPER'S QUARTERS
APOSTLE ISLANDS NATIONAL LAKESHORE   LaPOINTE VICINITY   ASHLAND COUNTY   WISCONSIN

SURVEY NO.
WI-318A

HISTORIC AMERICAN
BUILDINGS SURVEY
SHEET 5 OF 10 SHEETS

LIBRARY OF CONGRESS
INDEX NUMBER

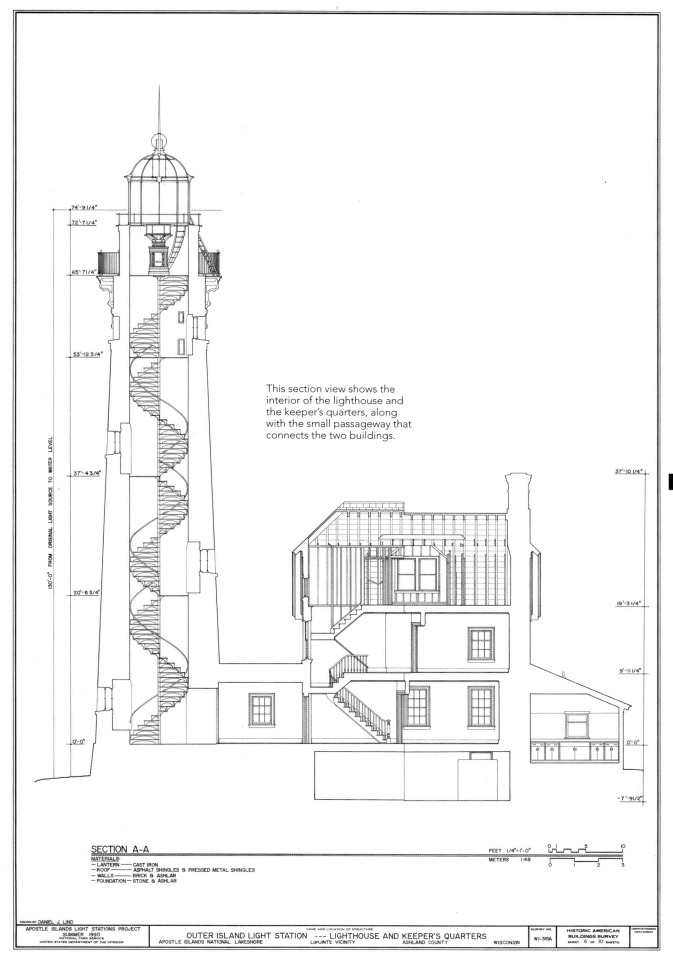

This section view shows the interior of the lighthouse and the keeper's quarters, along with the small passageway that connects the two buildings.

SECTION A-A

MATERIALS:
- LANTERN ———— CAST IRON
- ROOF ———— ASPHALT SHINGLES & PRESSED METAL SHINGLES
- WALLS ———— BRICK & ASHLAR
- FOUNDATION — STONE & ASHLAR

FEET 1/4"=1'-0"
METERS 1:48

DRAWN BY: DANIEL J. LIND

APOSTLE ISLANDS LIGHT STATIONS PROJECT
SUMMER 1990
NATIONAL PARK SERVICE
UNITED STATES DEPARTMENT OF THE INTERIOR

NAME AND LOCATION OF STRUCTURE
OUTER ISLAND LIGHT STATION --- LIGHTHOUSE AND KEEPER'S QUARTERS
APOSTLE ISLANDS NATIONAL LAKESHORE   LaPOINTE VICINITY   ASHLAND COUNTY   WISCONSIN

SURVEY NO.
WI-318A

HISTORIC AMERICAN BUILDINGS SURVEY
SHEET 6 OF 10 SHEETS

These plans show the first and
second floor of the keeper's
quarters, as well as the lighthouse.

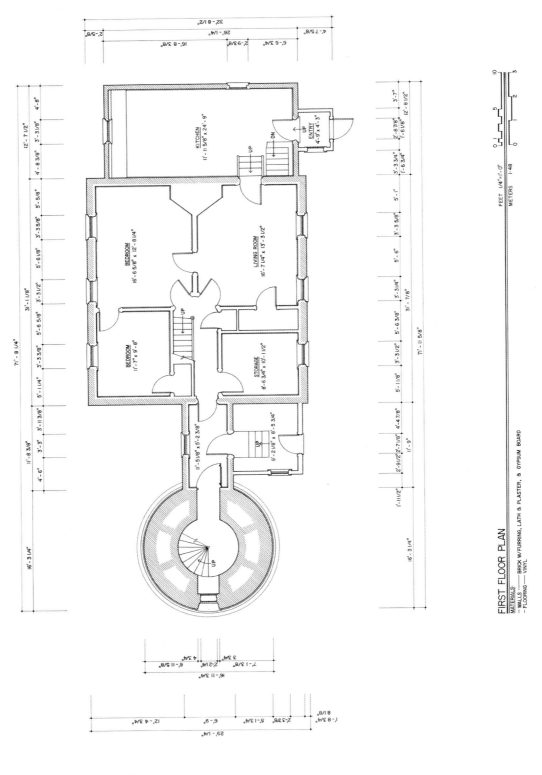

FIRST FLOOR PLAN

MATERIALS
- WALLS ——— BRICK w/ FURRING, LATH & PLASTER, & GYPSUM BOARD
- FLOORING ——— VINYL

FEET 1/4"=1'-0"
METERS 1:48

DRAWN BY: EVA H. KUNCKEL
APOSTLE ISLANDS LIGHT STATIONS PROJECT
SUMMER 1990
NATIONAL PARK SERVICE
UNITED STATES DEPARTMENT OF THE INTERIOR

NAME AND LOCATION OF STRUCTURE
OUTER ISLAND LIGHT STATION --- LIGHTHOUSE AND KEEPER'S QUARTERS
APOSTLE ISLANDS NATIONAL LAKESHORE   LaPOINTE VICINITY   ASHLAND COUNTY   WISCONSIN

SURVEY NO.
WI-318A

HISTORIC AMERICAN
BUILDINGS SURVEY
SHEET 2 OF 10 SHEETS

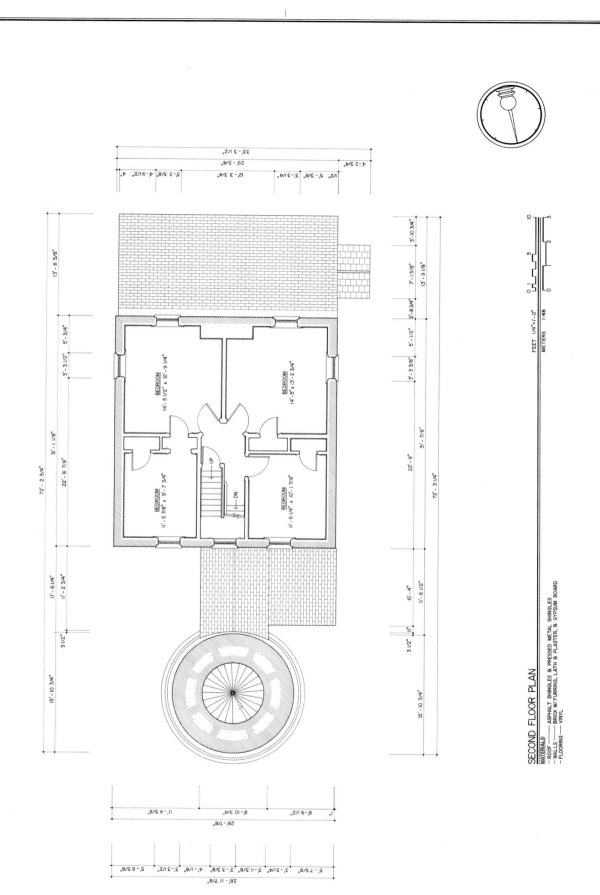

SECOND FLOOR PLAN

MATERIALS:
— ROOF —— ASPHALT SHINGLES & PRESSED METAL SHINGLES
— WALLS —— BRICK W/ FURRING, LATH & PLASTER, & GYPSUM BOARD
— FLOORING —— VINYL

DRAWN BY: KENNETH W. MARTIN
APOSTLE ISLANDS LIGHT STATIONS PROJECT
SUMMER 1990
NATIONAL PARK SERVICE
UNITED STATES DEPARTMENT OF THE INTERIOR

NAME AND LOCATION OF STRUCTURE
OUTER ISLAND LIGHT STATION --- LIGHTHOUSE AND KEEPER'S QUARTERS
APOSTLE ISLANDS NATIONAL LAKESHORE   LaPOINTE VICINITY   ASHLAND COUNTY   WISCONSIN

SURVEY NO.
WI-318A

HISTORIC AMERICAN
BUILDINGS SURVEY
SHEET 3 OF 10 SHEETS

The watch room, located
near the top of the tower,
is shown here.

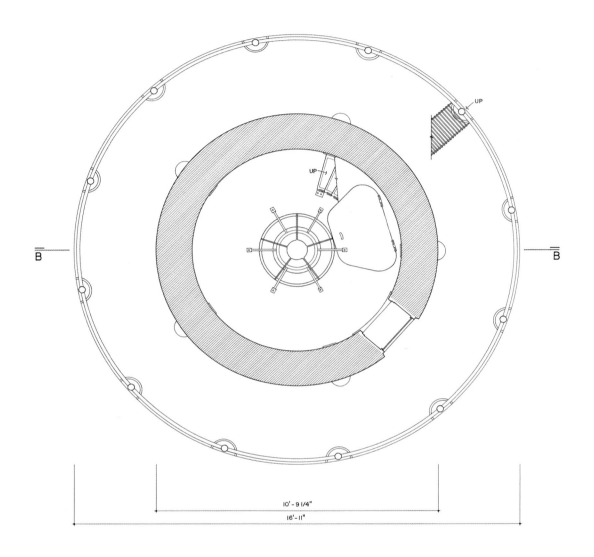

B — — B

10' - 9 1/4"

16' - 11"

WATCH ROOM PLAN

FEET   3/4" = 1' - 0"

METERS   1:16

MATERIALS:
— WALLS ——— BRICK
— BALCONY ——— CAST IRON

DRAWN BY: DANIEL J. LIND, INKED BY: JUDITH E. COLLINS
APOSTLE ISLANDS LIGHT STATIONS PROJECT
SUMMER 1990
NATIONAL PARK SERVICE
UNITED STATES DEPARTMENT OF THE INTERIOR

NAME AND LOCATION OF STRUCTURE
OUTER ISLAND LIGHT STATION --- LIGHTHOUSE AND KEEPER'S QUARTERS
APOSTLE ISLANDS NATIONAL LAKESHORE   LaPOINTE VICINITY   ASHLAND COUNTY   WISCONSIN

SURVEY NO.
WI-318A

HISTORIC AMERICAN
BUILDINGS SURVEY
SHEET 8 OF 10 SHEETS

LIBRARY OF CONGRESS
INDEX NUMBER

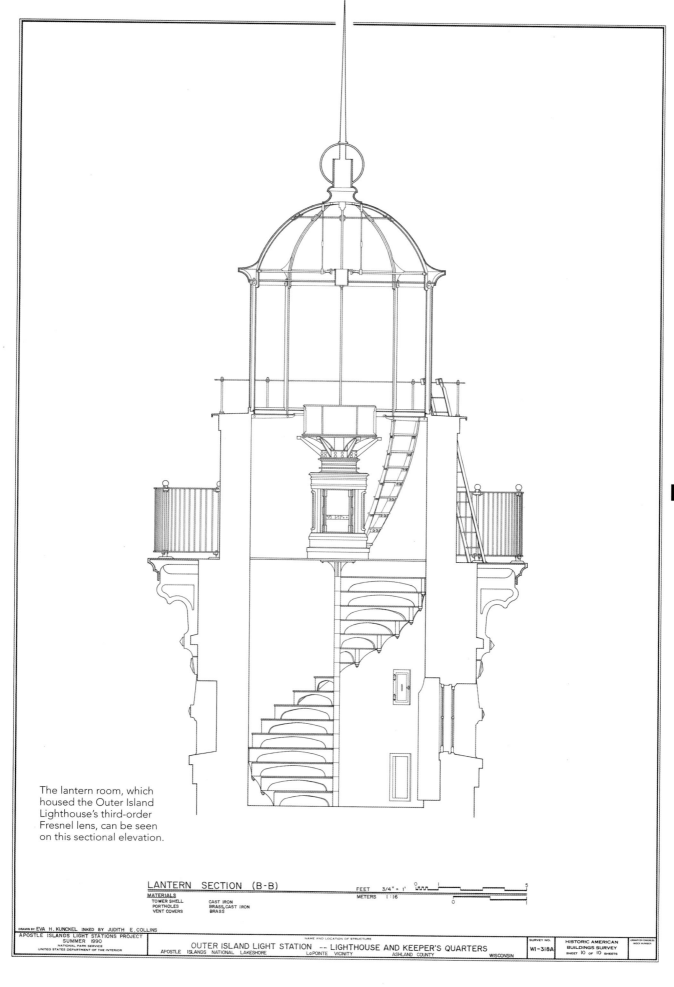

The lantern room, which housed the Outer Island Lighthouse's third-order Fresnel lens, can be seen on this sectional elevation.

LANTERN   SECTION   (B-B)

FEET   3/4" = 1'

METERS   1:16

MATERIALS

TOWER SHELL	CAST IRON
PORTHOLES	BRASS, CAST IRON
VENT COVERS	BRASS

DRAWN BY EVA H. KUNCKEL INKED BY JUDITH E. COLLINS

APOSTLE ISLANDS LIGHT STATIONS PROJECT
SUMMER 1990
NATIONAL PARK SERVICE
UNITED STATES DEPARTMENT OF THE INTERIOR

NAME AND LOCATION OF STRUCTURE

OUTER ISLAND LIGHT STATION -- LIGHTHOUSE AND KEEPER'S QUARTERS
APOSTLE ISLANDS NATIONAL LAKESHORE   LaPOINTE VICINITY   ASHLAND COUNTY   WISCONSIN

SURVEY NO.
WI-318A

HISTORIC AMERICAN
BUILDINGS SURVEY
SHEET 10 OF 10 SHEETS

LIBRARY OF CONGRESS
INDEX NUMBER

PENSACOLA LIGHTHOUSE

ESCAMBIA COUNTY, FLORIDA • ORIGINAL LIGHTHOUSE BUILT IN 1824

In addition to being Florida's second oldest city, Pensacola is located near the deepest bay off the Gulf of Mexico. After Florida fell under the control of the United States in the early 1800s, the government sought to utilize the bay and made plans to erect a lighthouse there. To aid with navigation while the new lighthouse tower was under construction, the *Aurora Borealis*, a floating lightship, was stationed in the bay. The lighthouse was completed in 1824 and used a gear system to rotate two sets of lamps, producing a flashing light. After concerns were voiced about the lighthouse being too short and its light too dim, a new tower was constructed under a mile away in 1858. The new tower was 160' tall and contained a first-order Fresnel lens. The lighthouse was used as a Confederate base during the Civil War and was actually struck several times by cannon fire from nearby Fort Pickens. After the war, the upper two-thirds of the tower were painted black to make it stand out against cloudy skies during the day. The tower was struck by lightning twice in 1874 and survived an earthquake in 1886. The lighthouse received an automated light in 1965.

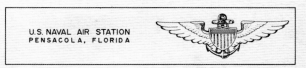

U.S. NAVAL AIR STATION
PENSACOLA, FLORIDA

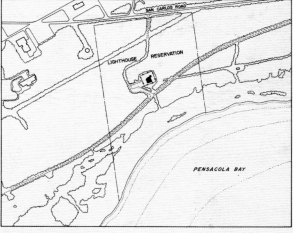

LOCATION MAP

0   200   400   800
SCALE IN FEET   1"= 400'

SOURCE: MASTER SHORE STATION DEVELOPMENT PLAN · YARDS AND DOCKS DRAWING NUMBER 686034

88

Pensacola Lighthouse Association

DRAWN BY TUCKER BISHOP 1972
HABS N.A.S. OFFICE
OFFICE OF ARCHEOLOGY AND HISTORIC PRESERVATION
UNDER DIRECTION OF THE NATIONAL PARK SERVICE
UNITED STATES DEPARTMENT OF THE INTERIOR

NAME AND LOCATION OF STRUCTURE
PENSACOLA LIGHTHOUSE
C.G. RESERVATION   NAVAL AIR STATION   PENSACOLA   ESCAMBIA COUNTY   FLORIDA

SURVEY NO.
FLA.
147

HISTORIC AMERICAN
BUILDINGS SURVEY
SHEET 1 OF 3 SHEETS

Shortly after the United States gained control of Florida, the Pensacola Lighthouse was built to guide ships into the Pensacola Bay, the deepest bay on the Gulf Coast.

This drawing provides an interior and exterior view of the lighthouse.

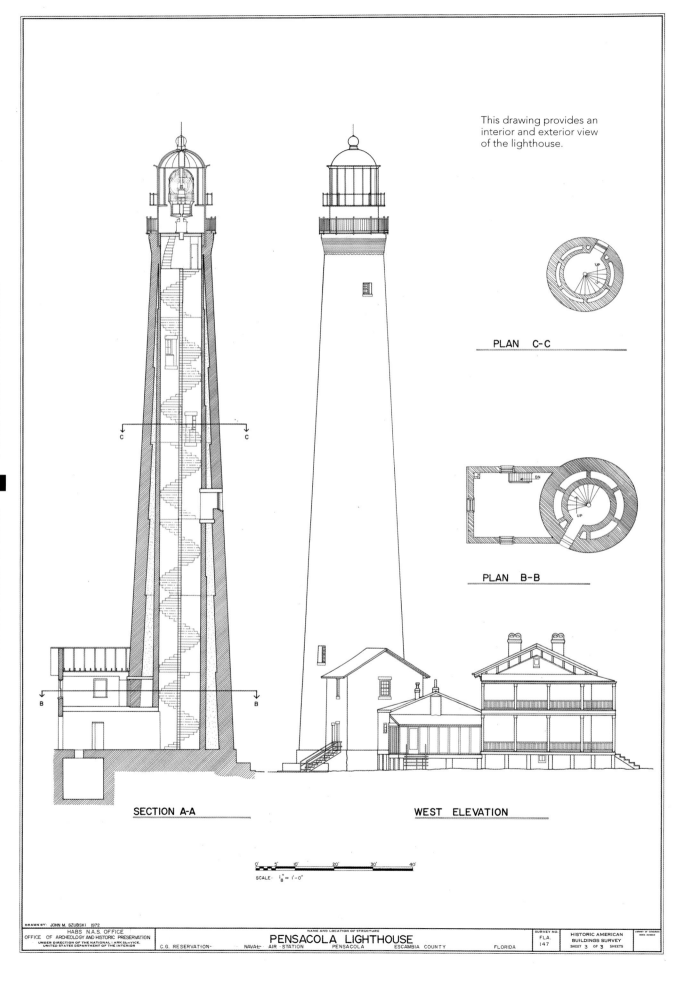

PLAN C-C

PLAN B-B

SECTION A-A

WEST ELEVATION

SCALE: $\frac{1}{8}" = 1'-0"$

DRAWN BY: JOHN M. SZUBSKI 1972
HABS N.A.S. OFFICE
OFFICE OF ARCHEOLOGY AND HISTORIC PRESERVATION
UNDER DIRECTION OF THE NATIONAL PARK SERVICE,
UNITED STATES DEPARTMENT OF THE INTERIOR

NAME AND LOCATION OF STRUCTURE
PENSACOLA LIGHTHOUSE
C.G. RESERVATION- NAVAL AIR STATION PENSACOLA ESCAMBIA COUNTY FLORIDA

SURVEY NO.
FLA.
147

HISTORIC AMERICAN
BUILDINGS SURVEY
SHEET 3 OF 3 SHEETS

HABS # FLA 147

The Pensacola Lighthouse was lit with a first-order Fresnel lens so that it could easily be seen by ships about 20 miles out to sea.

Confederate soldiers used the Pensacolia Lighthouse as a base during the Civil War. During that time, the tower was struck by Union cannon fire.

The lighthouse contains 177 steps that spiral from the base of the tower to the light above.

HABS # FLA 147

After the Civil War, the upper two-thirds of the lighthouse were painted black so that it would stand out against cloudy skies and could be used as a landmark during the day.

Today the Pensacola Lighthouse is maintained by the Pensacola Lighthouse Association and may be visited seven days a week, year-round.

PIGEON POINT LIGHTHOUSE

SAN MATEO COUNTY, CALIFORNIA
BUILT IN 1872

Pigeon Point, California, was named for the *Carrier Pigeon*, a ship that struck the point and sank during its maiden voyage in the 1850s. Several similar shipwrecks soon prompted the construction of a lighthouse. The brick tower was completed in October of 1872, and the 1,008-piece French-made first-order Fresnel lens was installed in November. The tower's light had originally been used in the Cape Hatteras Lighthouse, but was removed during the Civil War and installed at Pigeon Point. Pigeon Point Lighthouse and Point Arena Lighthouse both stand 115' tall, making them the tallest lighthouses on the West Coast. In 1943, a radio antenna was placed near the Pigeon Point Lighthouse. Ships used the Morse code signals emitted by the antenna and the sounds from the lighthouse fog signal to determine their location. The light was automated in 1974.

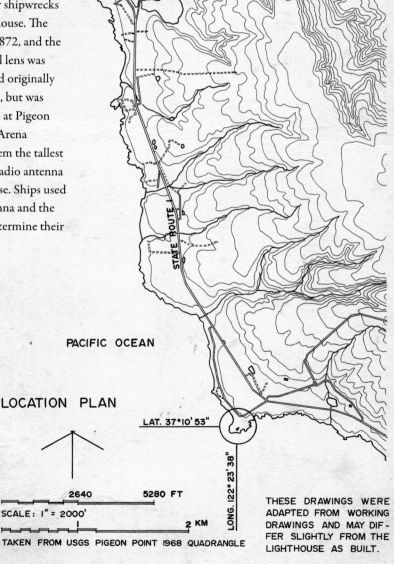

PACIFIC OCEAN

LOCATION PLAN

LAT. 37°10'53"

LONG. 122° 23' 38"

2640   5280 FT

SCALE : 1" = 2000'

2 KM

TAKEN FROM USGS PIGEON POINT 1968 QUADRANGLE

THESE DRAWINGS WERE ADAPTED FROM WORKING DRAWINGS AND MAY DIFFER SLIGHTLY FROM THE LIGHTHOUSE AS BUILT.

SAN MATEO COUNTY PROJECT 1974
OFFICE OF ARCHEOLOGY & HISTORIC PRESERVATION
UNDER DIRECTION OF THE NATIONAL PARK SERVICE.
UNITED STATES DEPARTMENT OF THE INTERIOR.

NAME AND LOCATION OF STRUCTURE
PIGEON POINT LIGHTHOUSE
NEAR STATE HIGHWAY 1   PESCADERO VICINITY   SAN MATEO COUNTY   CALIFORNIA

SURVEY NO.
CAL
1997

HISTORIC AMERICAN
BUILDINGS SURVEY
SHEET 1 OF 5 OF 6 SHEETS

LIBRARY OF CONGRESS
INDEX NUMBER

Pigeon Point was originally known as *Punta de las Ballenas*, or Point of the Whales, until the *Carrier Pigeon* was shipwrecked there in the 1850s.

LIGHTHOUSES: A CLOSE-UP LOOK

The Pigeon Point Lighthouse, pictured in the photos above, and the Point Arena Lighthouse are 115' tall, making them the tallest lighthouses on the West Coast.

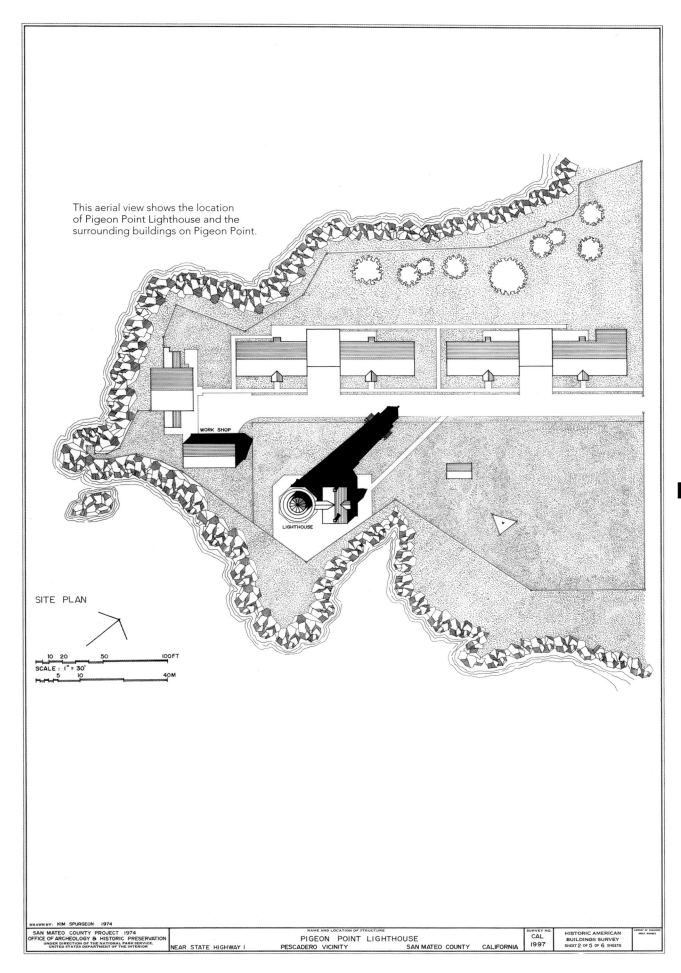

This aerial view shows the location of Pigeon Point Lighthouse and the surrounding buildings on Pigeon Point.

WORK SHOP

LIGHTHOUSE

SITE PLAN

10 20   50   100FT
SCALE : 1" = 30'
     5   10   40M

DRAWN BY: KIM SPURGEON 1974

SAN MATEO COUNTY PROJECT 1974 OFFICE OF ARCHEOLOGY & HISTORIC PRESERVATION UNDER DIRECTION OF THE NATIONAL PARK SERVICE. UNITED STATES DEPARTMENT OF THE INTERIOR	NAME AND LOCATION OF STRUCTURE PIGEON POINT LIGHTHOUSE	SURVEY NO. CAL 1997	HISTORIC AMERICAN BUILDINGS SURVEY SHEET 2 OF 5 OF 6 SHEETS	LIBRARY OF CONGRESS INDEX NUMBER
	NEAR STATE HIGHWAY I	PESCADERO VICINITY	SAN MATEO COUNTY	CALIFORNIA		

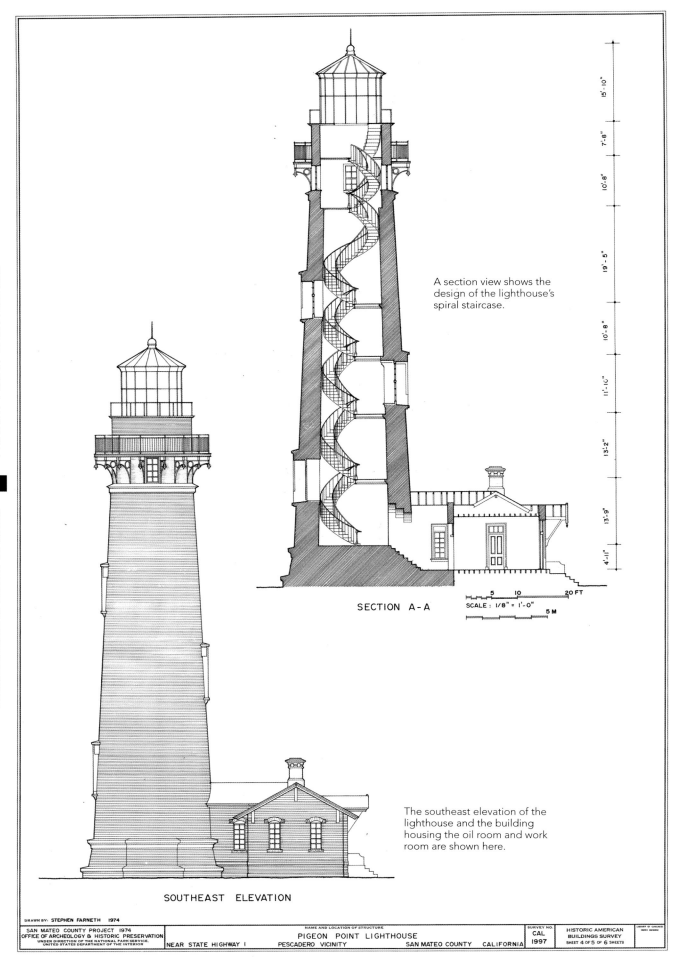

A section view shows the design of the lighthouse's spiral staircase.

SECTION A-A

SCALE: 1/8" = 1'-0"

5   10   20 FT

5 M

The southeast elevation of the lighthouse and the building housing the oil room and work room are shown here.

SOUTHEAST ELEVATION

DRAWN BY: STEPHEN FARNETH 1974

SAN MATEO COUNTY PROJECT 1974
OFFICE OF ARCHEOLOGY & HISTORIC PRESERVATION
UNDER DIRECTION OF THE NATIONAL PARK SERVICE,
UNITED STATES DEPARTMENT OF THE INTERIOR

NEAR STATE HIGHWAY 1

NAME AND LOCATION OF STRUCTURE
PIGEON POINT LIGHTHOUSE
PESCADERO VICINITY   SAN MATEO COUNTY   CALIFORNIA

SURVEY NO.
CAL
1997

HISTORIC AMERICAN
BUILDINGS SURVEY
SHEET 4 OF 5 OF 6 SHEETS

LIBRARY OF CONGRESS
INDEX NUMBER

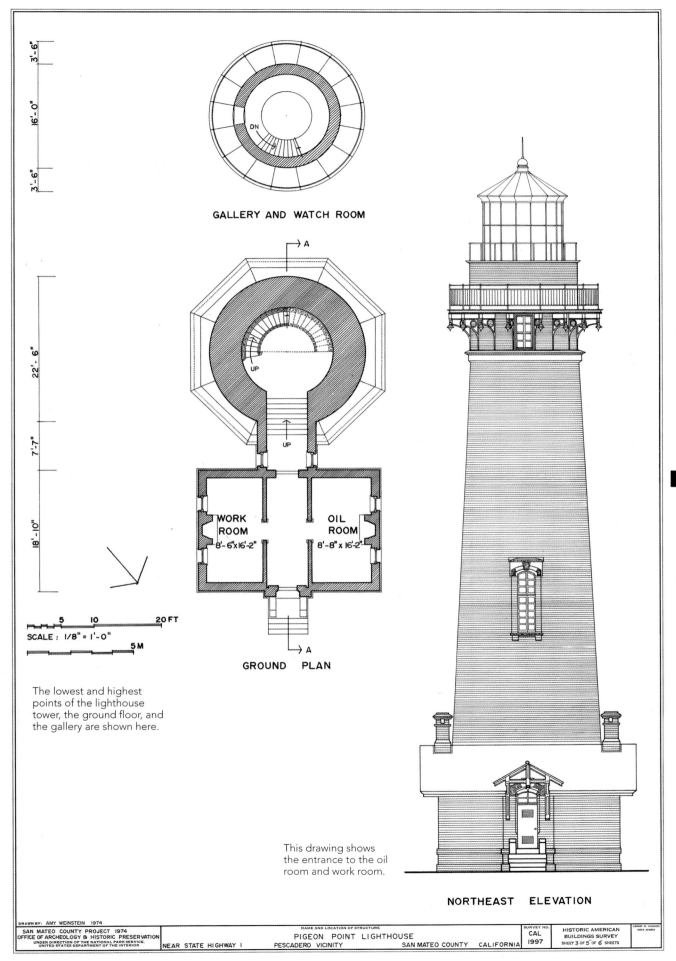

GALLERY AND WATCH ROOM

A

WORK
ROOM
8'-6"x16'-2"

OIL
ROOM
8'-8" x 16'-2"

UP

UP

DN

A

GROUND PLAN

3'-6"

16'-0"

3'-6"

22'-6"

7'-7"

18'-10"

5   10   20 FT

SCALE : 1/8" = 1'-0"

5 M

The lowest and highest
points of the lighthouse
tower, the ground floor, and
the gallery are shown here.

This drawing shows
the entrance to the oil
room and work room.

NORTHEAST ELEVATION

DRAWN BY: AMY WEINSTEIN 1974

| SAN MATEO COUNTY PROJECT 1974 OFFICE OF ARCHEOLOGY & HISTORIC PRESERVATION UNDER DIRECTION OF THE NATIONAL PARK SERVICE. UNITED STATES DEPARTMENT OF THE INTERIOR | NAME AND LOCATION OF STRUCTURE PIGEON POINT LIGHTHOUSE | SURVEY NO. CAL 1997 | HISTORIC AMERICAN BUILDINGS SURVEY | LIBRARY OF CONGRESS INDEX NUMBER |
| | NEAR STATE HIGHWAY 1 PESCADERO VICINITY SAN MATEO COUNTY CALIFORNIA | | SHEET 3 OF 5 OF 6 SHEETS | |

The Pigeon Point keeper
regularly climbed the
tower's 136 stairs.

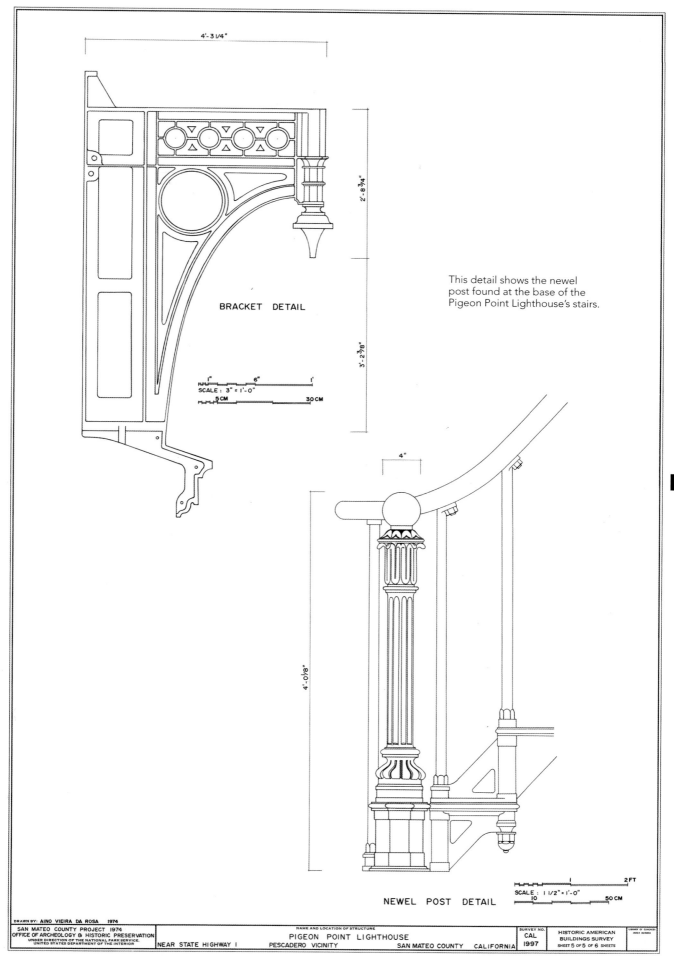

4'-3 1/4"

2'-8 3/4"

3'-2 3/8"

BRACKET DETAIL

1" 6" 1'
SCALE : 3" = 1'-0"
5 CM   30 CM

This detail shows the newel
post found at the base of the
Pigeon Point Lighthouse's stairs.

4"

4'-0 1/8"

NEWEL POST DETAIL

2 FT
SCALE : 1 1/2" = 1'-0"
10   50 CM

DRAWN BY: AINO VIEIRA DA ROSA 1974

SAN MATEO COUNTY PROJECT 1974
OFFICE OF ARCHEOLOGY & HISTORIC PRESERVATION
UNDER DIRECTION OF THE NATIONAL PARK SERVICE.
UNITED STATES DEPARTMENT OF THE INTERIOR

NAME AND LOCATION OF STRUCTURE
PIGEON POINT LIGHTHOUSE
NEAR STATE HIGHWAY 1   PESCADERO VICINITY   SAN MATEO COUNTY   CALIFORNIA

SURVEY NO.
CAL
1997

HISTORIC AMERICAN
BUILDINGS SURVEY
SHEET 5 OF 5 OF 6 SHEETS

LIBRARY OF CONGRESS
INDEX NUMBER

104

The Pigeon Point Lighthouse tower is made of brick and is attached to a small building that houses an oil room and a work room.

The lighthouse's first-order Fresnel lens was made up of 1,008 individual prisms.

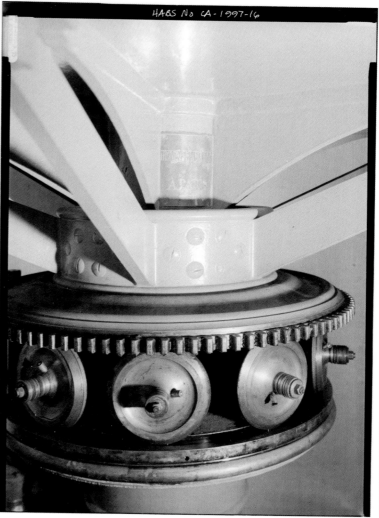

In 1943, a radio antenna was placed near the lighthouse. The antenna emitted Morse code signals that sailors could match with the sounding of the fog signal to determine how close they were to shore.

Although the Pigeon Point Lighthouse is not damaged in this photo, sections of the cornice fell off in 2001, resulting in efforts to restore the tower to its original condition.

Point (Port) Isabel Lighthouse

Cameron County, Texas
Built in 1853

The Point or Port Isabel Lighthouse was completed around 1853. It was used to guide ships through the Brazos Santiago Pass, a narrow waterway that passes between Padre Island and Brazos Island. Ships needed to navigate this pass to reach the mouth of the Rio Grande River, where they would offload goods to be transported inland. Previously, buoys had been used to mark the water way, but after Texas became a state in 1845, its citizens called for a lighthouse. The construction of the tower was completed in 1852, but the ship carrying the parts for the stairwell and the lantern room from New York to Texas was shipwrecked, delaying the completion of the full structure. The light first shone from Port Isabel in March 1853.

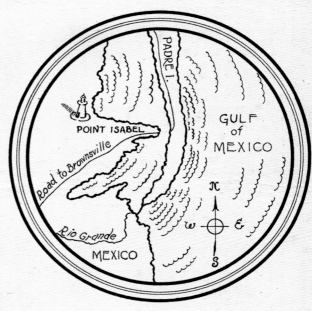

108

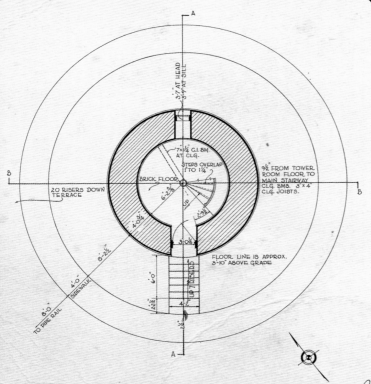

HISTORIC AMERICAN BUILDINGS SURVEY
U.S. DEPARTMENT OF THE INTERIOR
NATIONAL PARK SERVICE
BRANCH OF PLANS AND DESIGN

MEASURED: MARCH, 19, 1934
DRAWN: APRIL, 29, 1936
MEASUREMENTS CHECKED: CHARLES BERTRAND

DRAWINGS APPROVED:
DRAWINGS APPROVED:
ACCEPTED FOR LIBRARY OF CONGRESS:

DISTRICT OFFICER

CHIEF ARCHITECT.

* DISTRICT OFFICER *
BARTLETT COCKE
615 MAVERICK BLDG.
SAN ANTONIO - TEXAS
* FIELD PARTY *
BARTLETT COCKE & ANTON HEISLER

SURVEY NO.
33-AB-1
SHEETS
1 TO 4

INDEX NO.
TEX
31. P9/oA

The Point Isabel Lighthouse was constructed in Texas to guide ships into the Rio Grande River.

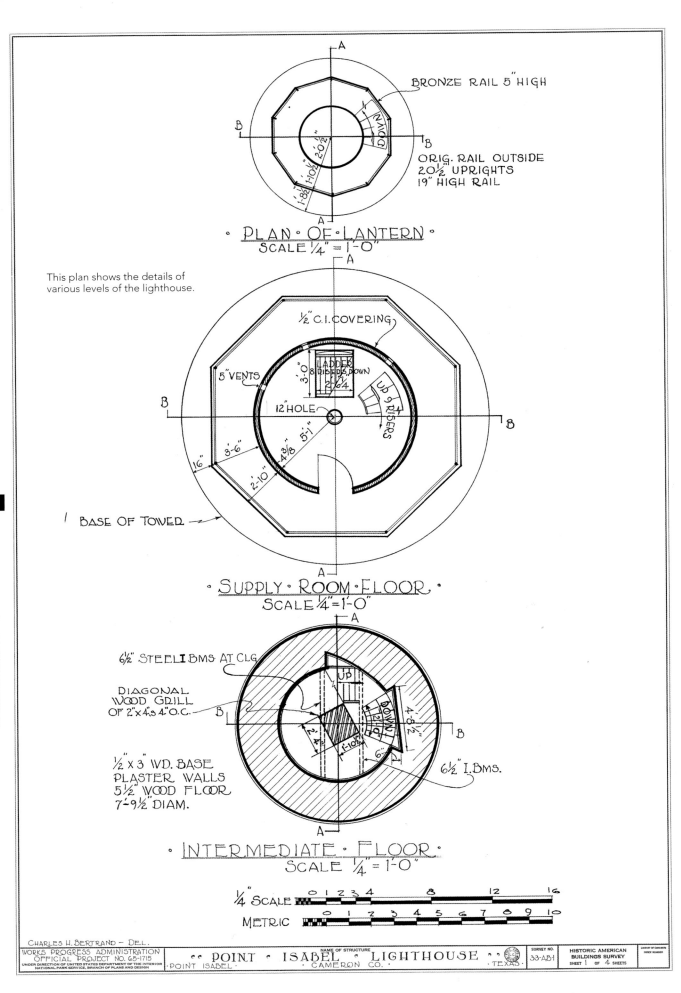

This plan shows the details of various levels of the lighthouse.

BRONZE RAIL 5" HIGH

ORIG. RAIL OUTSIDE
20½ UPRIGHTS
19" HIGH RAIL

• PLAN • OF • LANTERN •
SCALE ¼" = 1'-0"

½" C.I. COVERING

5" VENTS

LADDER
8 RISERS DOWN

12" HOLE

UP 9 RISERS

BASE OF TOWER

• SUPPLY • ROOM • FLOOR •
SCALE ¼" = 1'-0"

6½" STEEL I BMS AT CLG

DIAGONAL
WOOD GRILL
OF 2" x 4" 3'4" O.C.

½" x 3" WD. BASE
PLASTER WALLS
5½" WOOD FLOOR
7'-9½" DIAM.

UP

DOWN

6½" I. BMS.

• INTERMEDIATE • FLOOR •
SCALE ¼" = 1'-0"

¼" SCALE   0 1 2 3 4   8   12   16

METRIC   0 1 2 3 4 5 6 7 8 9 10

CHARLES H. BERTRAND — DEL.

WORKS PROGRESS ADMINISTRATION
OFFICIAL PROJECT NO. 65-1715
UNDER DIRECTION OF UNITED STATES DEPARTMENT OF THE INTERIOR
NATIONAL PARK SERVICE, BRANCH OF PLANS AND DESIGN

NAME OF STRUCTURE
•• POINT • ISABEL • LIGHTHOUSE ••
• POINT ISABEL •   • CAMERON CO. •   • TEXAS •

SURVEY NO.
33-AB-1

HISTORIC AMERICAN
BUILDINGS SURVEY
SHEET 1 OF 4 SHEETS

LIBRARY OF CONGRESS
INDEX NUMBER

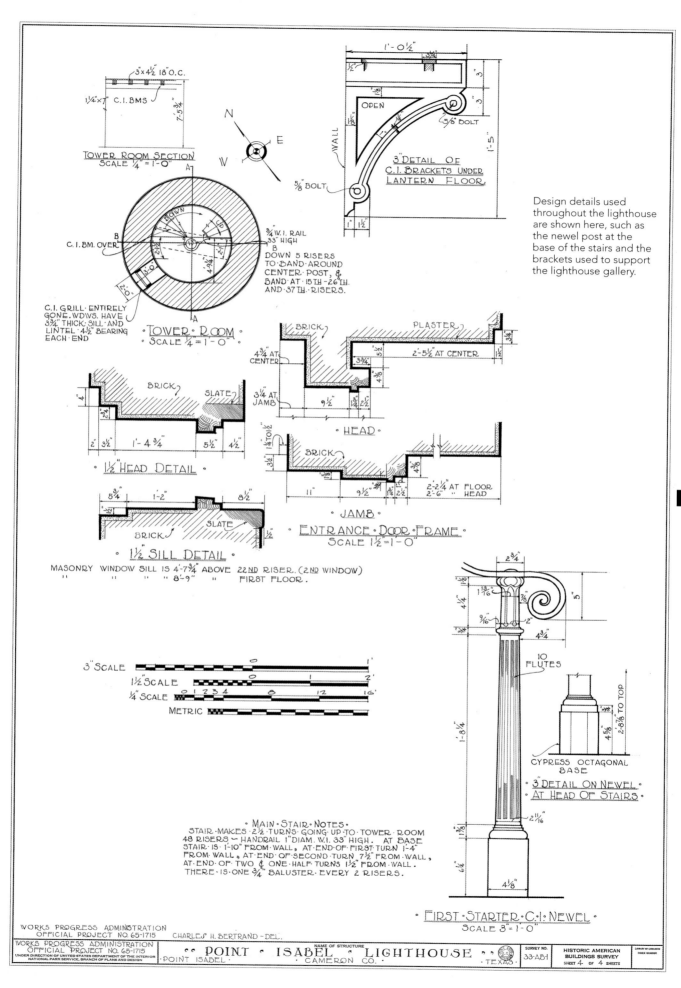

3x4½ 18 O.C.

1¼"×7" C.I. BMS

7-3¾

TOWER ROOM SECTION
SCALE ¼" = 1'-0"

N
E
W

3"DETAIL OF
C.I. BRACKETS UNDER
LANTERN FLOOR

1'-0½"
¾
½
3"
3"

OPEN
WALL
1⅛"
⅝" BOLT
1'-5"
1"   1½"

5/8" BOLT

Design details used
throughout the lighthouse
are shown here, such as
the newel post at the
base of the stairs and the
brackets used to support
the lighthouse gallery.

C.I. BM. OVER
DOWN
UP
B   B
3-0
2-0

¾" W.I. RAIL
33" HIGH
DOWN 5 RISERS
TO BAND AROUND
CENTER POST, &
BAND AT 15TH-26TH.
AND 37TH RISERS.

C.I. GRILL ENTIRELY
GONE. WDWS. HAVE
3¾" THICK SILL AND
LINTEL 4½" BEARING
EACH END

TOWER ROOM
SCALE ¼" = 1'-0"

BRICK
SLATE
4"
2" 3½ 1'-4¾" 5½" 4½"

1½" HEAD DETAIL

BRICK
PLASTER
4¾ AT CENTER
3¾
5½
2-5½ AT CENTER
3¾
9½"

HEAD

BRICK
1'4 TO ½
11"
9½"
2-2¼ AT FLOOR
2-6" HEAD

JAMB

5¾ 1'-2" 8½"
BRICK   SLATE
½

1½ SILL DETAIL

ENTRANCE DOOR FRAME
SCALE 1½" = 1'-0"

MASONRY WINDOW SILL IS 4'-7¾" ABOVE 22ND RISER. (2ND WINDOW)
"   "   "   "   8'-9"   "   FIRST FLOOR.

3" SCALE
0   1'
1½" SCALE
0   1'   2'
¼" SCALE
0 1 2 3 4   8   12   16'
METRIC

2¾
1¹³⁄₁₆
4¼
9⁄16
2
5
4¾
10 FLUTES

1'-8¾"
2-8⅞ TO TOP
4⅝
CYPRESS OCTAGONAL BASE

3" DETAIL ON NEWEL
AT HEAD OF STAIRS

MAIN STAIR NOTES
STAIR MAKES 2½ TURNS GOING UP TO TOWER ROOM
48 RISERS ~ HANDRAIL 1"DIAM. W.I. 33" HIGH. AT BASE
STAIR IS 1'-10" FROM WALL, AT END OF FIRST TURN 1'-4"
FROM WALL, AT END OF SECOND TURN 7½" FROM WALL,
AT END OF TWO & ONE HALF TURNS 1½" FROM WALL.
THERE IS ONE ¾" BALUSTER EVERY 2 RISERS.

1¾
6¼
2¹¹⁄₁₆
4⅛

FIRST STARTER C.I. NEWEL
SCALE 3" = 1'-0"

WORKS PROGRESS ADMINISTRATION
OFFICIAL PROJECT NO. 65-1715
CHARLES H. BERTRAND - DEL.

WORKS PROGRESS ADMINISTRATION
OFFICIAL PROJECT NO. 65-1715
UNDER DIRECTION OF UNITED STATES DEPARTMENT OF THE INTERIOR
NATIONAL PARK SERVICE, BRANCH OF PLANS AND DESIGN

NAME OF STRUCTURE
POINT ISABEL LIGHTHOUSE
POINT ISABEL · CAMERON CO. · TEXAS

SURVEY NO.
33-ABI

HISTORIC AMERICAN
BUILDINGS SURVEY
SHEET 4 OF 4 SHEETS

LIBRARY OF CONGRESS
INDEX NUMBER

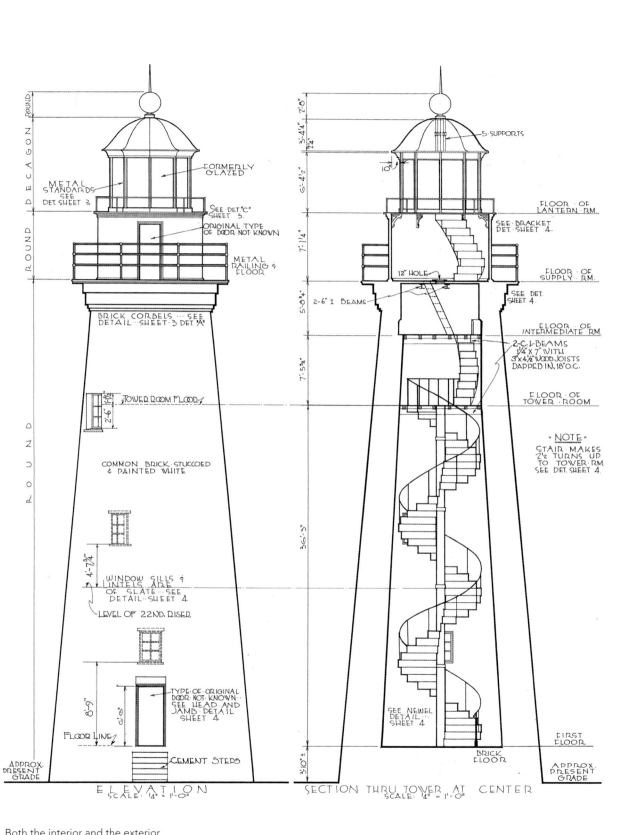

Both the interior and the exterior
of the lighthouse can be seen here.

113

The Point Isabel
Lighthouse was
restored in 2000.

Kraig Anderson

POINT REYES LIGHTHOUSE

MARIN COUNTY, CALIFORNIA
BUILT IN 1870

The Point Reyes Lighthouse was built to protect ships entering and leaving the San Francisco Bay from the Point Reyes Headlands, located 10 miles offshore. The lighthouse and fog signal were built on the cliffs at the very edge of the point. In order to reach the lighthouse, keepers would have to climb the 300 stairs that led up the cliff from their quarters to the tower. To reach the fog signal building, keepers faced about 330 more steps. The lighthouse's first-order Fresnel lens was assembled in France in 1867 before travelling to its new location on the California coast. It first shone on December 1, 1870.

The lighthouse remained incredibly reliable for the next 105 years, surviving wind gusts of over 100 miles an hour, severe storms, and an earthquake that moved the entire Point Reyes Peninsula, along with the lighthouse, 18' north. Although the light was automated in 1975, the Fresnel lens and the mechanism used to operate it were not removed from the lighthouse. After it was automated, the Point Reyes Lighthouse and the surrounding buildings were restored and are now part of the Point Reyes National Seashore.

DRAWN BY: B. SANTOS & N. CAMARENA

DENVER SERVICE CENTER
OFFICE OF ARCHEOLOGY AND HISTORIC PRESERVATION
UNDER DIRECTION OF THE NATIONAL PARK SERVICE
UNITED STATES DEPARTMENT OF THE INTERIOR

NAME AND LOCATION OF STRUCTURE
POINT REYES LIGHTHOUSE
POINT REYES NATIONAL SEASHORE, MARIN COUNTY, CALIFORNIA

SURVEY NO.
CA-2250

HISTORIC AMERICAN
BUILDINGS SURVEY
SHEET 1 OF 5 SHEETS

The Point Reyes Lighthouse was built to help ships navigate around the Point Reyes Headlands, located near the entrance of the San Francisco Bay.

The Point Reyes Lighthouse is located on a segment of the California coast that juts out into the sea and was the site of the West Coast's first recorded shipwreck.

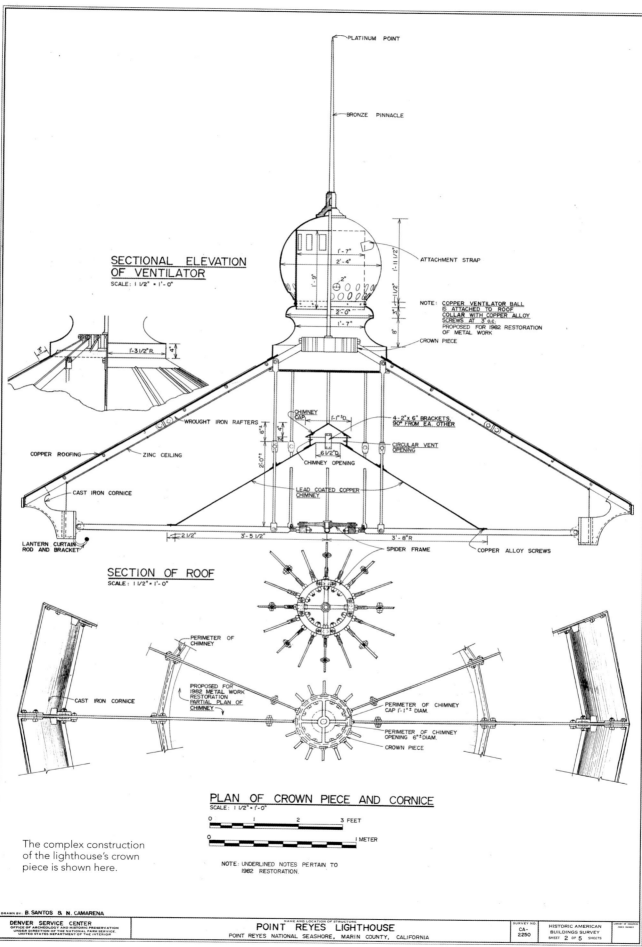

PLATINUM POINT

BRONZE PINNACLE

SECTIONAL ELEVATION
OF VENTILATOR
SCALE: 1 1/2" = 1'-0"

1'-7"
2'-4"
1'-9"
1'-11 1/2"
ATTACHMENT STRAP
2"
1 1/2"
2'-0"
3"
1'-7"
8"

NOTE: COPPER VENTILATOR BALL
IS ATTACHED TO ROOF
COLLAR WITH COPPER ALLOY
SCREWS AT 3" O.C.
PROPOSED FOR 1982 RESTORATION
OF METAL WORK

CROWN PIECE

3"
1'-3 1/2"R.
4"

WROUGHT IRON RAFTERS
COPPER ROOFING
ZINC CEILING
CAST IRON CORNICE

CHIMNEY
CAP
1'-1"±D.
6"±
4"±
2'-0"±
CHIMNEY OPENING

4-2"x 6" BRACKETS,
90° FROM EA. OTHER
CIRCULAR VENT
OPENING
6 1/2"D.
LEAD COATED COPPER
CHIMNEY

LANTERN CURTAIN
ROD AND BRACKET

SECTION OF ROOF
SCALE: 1 1/2" = 1'-0"

2 1/2"
3'-5 1/2"
SPIDER FRAME
3'-8"R
COPPER ALLOY SCREWS

PERIMETER OF
CHIMNEY

CAST IRON CORNICE

PROPOSED FOR
1982 METAL WORK
RESTORATION
PARTIAL PLAN OF
CHIMNEY

PERIMETER OF CHIMNEY
CAP 1'-1"± DIAM.

PERIMETER OF CHIMNEY
OPENING 6"± DIAM.

CROWN PIECE

PLAN OF CROWN PIECE AND CORNICE
SCALE: 1 1/2" = 1'-0"

0   1   2   3 FEET

0   1 METER

The complex construction
of the lighthouse's crown
piece is shown here.

NOTE: UNDERLINED NOTES PERTAIN TO
1982 RESTORATION.

DRAWN BY: B. SANTOS & N. CAMARENA

DENVER SERVICE CENTER
OFFICE OF ARCHEOLOGY AND HISTORIC PRESERVATION
UNDER DIRECTION OF THE NATIONAL PARK SERVICE
UNITED STATES DEPARTMENT OF THE INTERIOR

NAME AND LOCATION OF STRUCTURE
POINT REYES LIGHTHOUSE
POINT REYES NATIONAL SEASHORE, MARIN COUNTY, CALIFORNIA

SURVEY NO.
CA-
2250

HISTORIC AMERICAN
BUILDINGS SURVEY
SHEET 2 OF 5 SHEETS

612/25,002

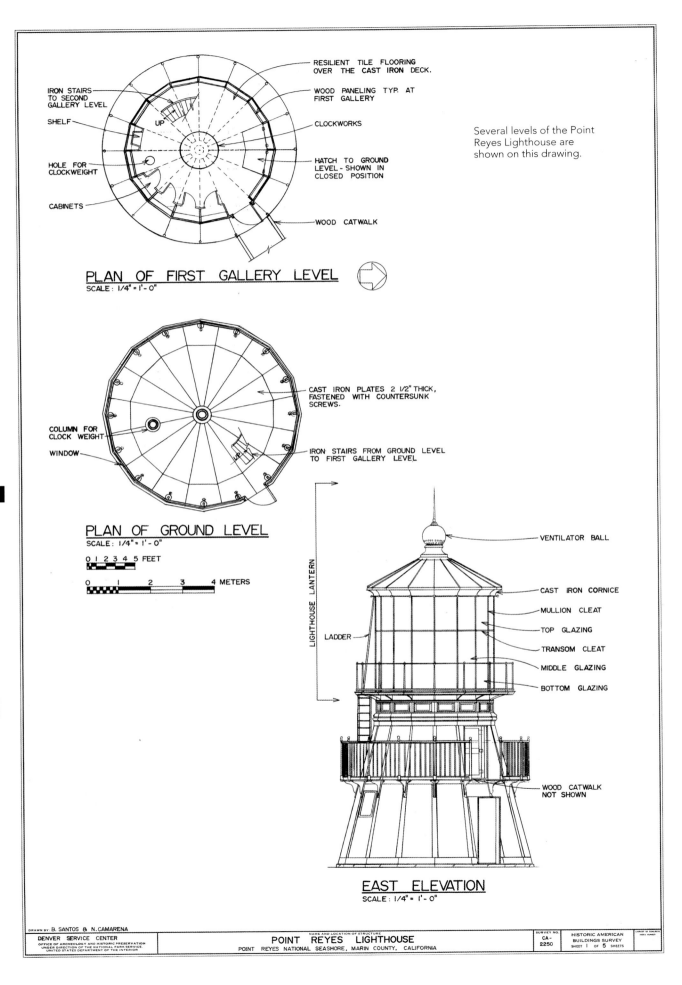

RESILIENT TILE FLOORING
OVER THE CAST IRON DECK.

WOOD PANELING TYP. AT
FIRST GALLERY

IRON STAIRS
TO SECOND
GALLERY LEVEL

SHELF

CLOCKWORKS

HATCH TO GROUND
LEVEL - SHOWN IN
CLOSED POSITION

HOLE FOR
CLOCKWEIGHT

CABINETS

WOOD CATWALK

UP

PLAN OF FIRST GALLERY LEVEL
SCALE: 1/4" = 1'- 0"

Several levels of the Point
Reyes Lighthouse are
shown on this drawing.

CAST IRON PLATES 2 1/2" THICK,
FASTENED WITH COUNTERSUNK
SCREWS.

COLUMN FOR
CLOCK WEIGHT

WINDOW

IRON STAIRS FROM GROUND LEVEL
TO FIRST GALLERY LEVEL

PLAN OF GROUND LEVEL
SCALE: 1/4" = 1'- 0"

0 1 2 3 4 5 FEET

0   1   2   3   4 METERS

VENTILATOR BALL

CAST IRON CORNICE

MULLION CLEAT

TOP GLAZING

TRANSOM CLEAT

MIDDLE GLAZING

BOTTOM GLAZING

LIGHTHOUSE LANTERN

LADDER

WOOD CATWALK
NOT SHOWN

EAST ELEVATION
SCALE: 1/4" = 1'- 0"

DRAWN BY: B. SANTOS & N. CAMARENA

DENVER SERVICE CENTER
OFFICE OF ARCHEOLOGY AND HISTORIC PRESERVATION
UNDER DIRECTION OF THE NATIONAL PARK SERVICE.
UNITED STATES DEPARTMENT OF THE INTERIOR

NAME AND LOCATION OF STRUCTURE

POINT REYES LIGHTHOUSE
POINT REYES NATIONAL SEASHORE, MARIN COUNTY, CALIFORNIA

SURVEY NO.
CA-
2250

HISTORIC AMERICAN
BUILDINGS SURVEY
SHEET 1 OF 5 SHEETS

LIBRARY OF CONGRESS
INDEX NUMBER

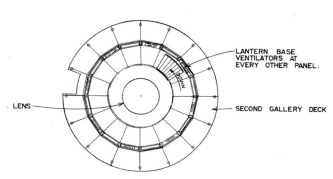

LANTERN BASE
VENTILATORS AT
EVERY OTHER PANEL.

LENS

SECOND GALLERY DECK

PLAN OF SECOND GALLERY LEVEL

SCALE : 1/4" = 1'-0"

This drawing shows the
placement of the light in the
lantern room.

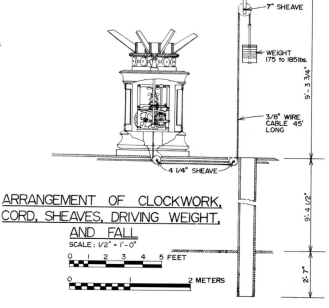

7" SHEAVE

WEIGHT
175 to 185 lbs.

9'- 3-3/4"

3/8" WIRE
CABLE 45'
LONG

4 1/4" SHEAVE

9'- 4 1/2"

2'- 7"

ARRANGEMENT OF CLOCKWORK,
CORD, SHEAVES, DRIVING WEIGHT,
AND FALL
SCALE : 1/2" = 1'-0"

0 1 2 3 4 5 FEET

0   1   2 METERS

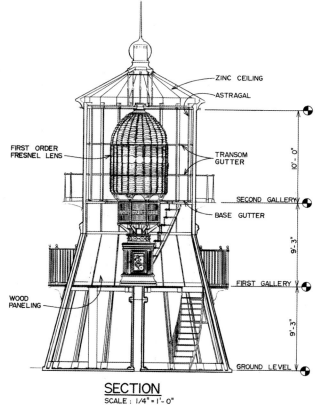

ZINC CEILING

ASTRAGAL

FIRST ORDER
FRESNEL LENS

TRANSOM
GUTTER

SECOND GALLERY

BASE GUTTER

10'-0"

FIRST GALLERY

9'-3"

WOOD
PANELING

9'-3"

GROUND LEVEL

SECTION
SCALE : 1/4" = 1'-0"

DRAWN BY: B. SANTOS & N. CAMARENA

DENVER SERVICE CENTER
OFFICE OF ARCHEOLOGY AND HISTORIC PRESERVATION
UNDER DIRECTION OF THE NATIONAL PARK SERVICE.
UNITED STATES DEPARTMENT OF THE INTERIOR

NAME AND LOCATION OF STRUCTURE
POINT REYES LIGHTHOUSE
POINT REYES NATIONAL SEASHORE, MARIN COUNTY, CALIFORNIA

SURVEY NO.
CA-
2250

HISTORIC AMERICAN
BUILDINGS SURVEY
SHEET 1 OF 5 SHEETS

Minute details found throughout the lighthouse, such as a curtain hook and a wall plate are shown on this drawing.

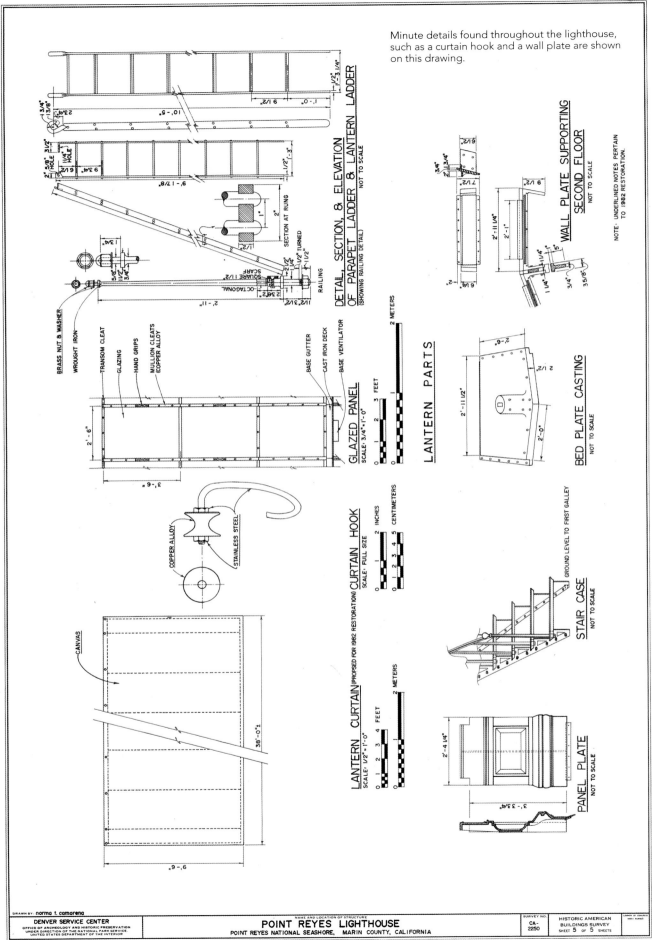

NOTE: UNDERLINED NOTES PERTAIN TO 1982 RESTORATION.

WALL PLATE SUPPORTING SECOND FLOOR
NOT TO SCALE

DETAIL, SECTION, & ELEVATION OF PARAPET LADDER & LANTERN LADDER
(SHOWING RAILING DETAIL) NOT TO SCALE

LANTERN PARTS

BED PLATE CASTING
NOT TO SCALE

GLAZED PANEL
SCALE: 3/4" = 1'-0"

STAIR CASE
NOT TO SCALE

LANTERN CURTAIN (PROPOSED FOR 1982 RESTORATION)
SCALE: 1/2" = 1'-0"

CURTAIN HOOK
SCALE: FULL SIZE

PANEL PLATE
NOT TO SCALE

DRAWN BY: norma t. camarena

DENVER SERVICE CENTER
OFFICE OF ARCHEOLOGY AND HISTORIC PRESERVATION
UNDER DIRECTION OF THE NATIONAL PARK SERVICE.
UNITED STATES DEPARTMENT OF THE INTERIOR

NAME AND LOCATION OF STRUCTURE
POINT REYES LIGHTHOUSE
POINT REYES NATIONAL SEASHORE, MARIN COUNTY, CALIFORNIA

SURVEY NO.
CA-2250

HISTORIC AMERICAN BUILDINGS SURVEY
SHEET 5 OF 5 SHEETS

612/25.002

Although the lighthouse itself is only 37' tall and does not contain many stairs, keepers had to climb 300 steps from the keeper's quarters to reach the lighthouse and about 330 more to reach the fog signal building.

Point Reyes was lit with a first-order Fresnel lens that was built in France in 1867.

The Fresnel Lens was turned by a gear system similar to that found in a clock.

HABS No. CA-2250-8

Although the lighthouse was automated in 1975, the light, which
had guided sailors for 105 years, remained in place.

The drawings on these pages show the details of the construction of the Point Reyes Lighthouse's cornice and gallery.

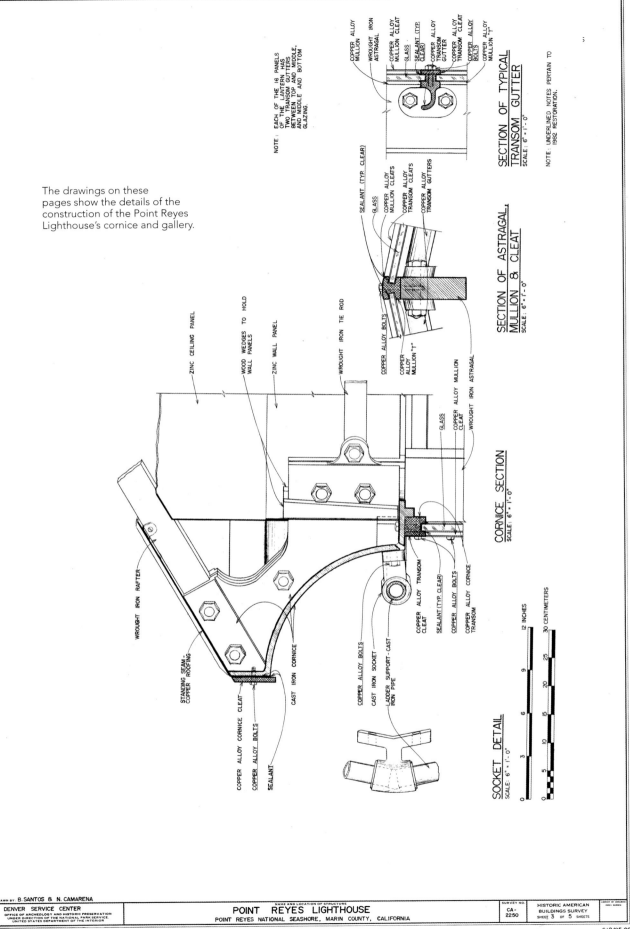

NOTE: EACH OF THE 16 PANELS OF THE LANTERN HAS TWO TRANSOM GUTTERS BETWEEN TOP AND MIDDLE AND MIDDLE AND BOTTOM GLAZING.

COPPER ALLOY MULLION
WROUGHT IRON ASTRAGAL
COPPER ALLOY MULLION CLEAT
SEALANT (TYP CLEAR)
GLASS
COPPER ALLOY TRANSOM GUTTER
COPPER ALLOY TRANSOM CLEAT
COPPER ALLOY BOLTS
COPPER ALLOY MULLION "T"

SECTION OF TYPICAL TRANSOM GUTTER
SCALE: 6" = 1'-0"

NOTE: UNDERLINED NOTES PERTAIN TO 1982 RESTORATION.

SEALANT (TYP. CLEAR)
GLASS
COPPER ALLOY MULLION CLEATS
COPPER ALLOY TRANSOM CLEATS
COPPER ALLOY TRANSOM GUTTERS
COPPER ALLOY BOLTS
COPPER ALLOY MULLION "T"
WROUGHT IRON ASTRAGAL

SECTION OF ASTRAGAL, MULLION & CLEAT
SCALE: 6" = 1'-0"

ZINC CEILING PANEL
WOOD WEDGES TO HOLD WALL PANELS
ZINC WALL PANEL
WROUGHT IRON TIE ROD

GLASS
COPPER ALLOY MULLION CLEAT
WROUGHT IRON ASTRAGAL

CORNICE SECTION
SCALE: 6" = 1'-0"

WROUGHT IRON RAFTER

STANDING SEAM - COPPER ROOFING

COPPER ALLOY CORNICE CLEAT
COPPER ALLOY BOLTS
SEALANT

CAST IRON CORNICE

COPPER ALLOY BOLTS
CAST IRON SOCKET
LADDER SUPPORT - CAST IRON PIPE

COPPER ALLOY TRANSOM CLEAT
SEALANT (TYP. CLEAR)
COPPER ALLOY BOLTS
COPPER ALLOY CORNICE TRANSOM

SOCKET DETAIL
SCALE: 6" = 1'-0"

0 3 6 9 12 INCHES
0 5 10 15 20 25 30 CENTIMETERS

DRAWN BY: B. SANTOS & N. CAMARENA

DENVER SERVICE CENTER
OFFICE OF ARCHEOLOGY AND HISTORIC PRESERVATION
UNDER DIRECTION OF THE NATIONAL PARK SERVICE
UNITED STATES DEPARTMENT OF THE INTERIOR

NAME AND LOCATION OF STRUCTURE
POINT REYES LIGHTHOUSE
POINT REYES NATIONAL SEASHORE, MARIN COUNTY, CALIFORNIA

SURVEY NO.
CA-2250

HISTORIC AMERICAN BUILDINGS SURVEY
SHEET 3 OF 5 SHEETS

LIBRARY OF CONGRESS

612/25,002

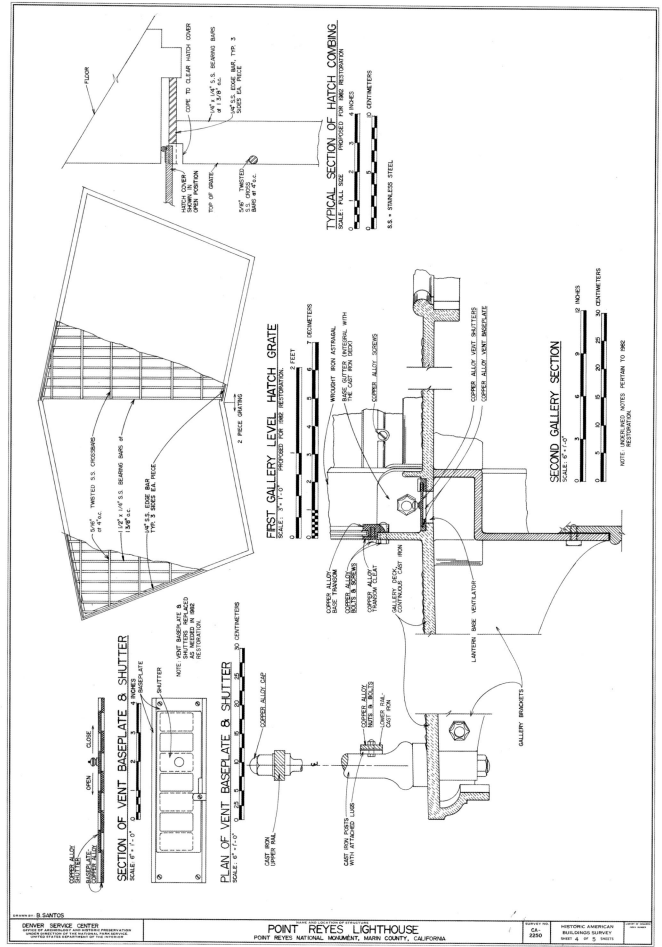

TYPICAL SECTION OF HATCH COMBING
SCALE: FULL SIZE   PROPOSED FOR 1982 RESTORATION.

S.S. = STAINLESS STEEL

FLOOR

COPE TO CLEAR HATCH COVER

1/4" S.S. BEARING BARS
at 1 3/8" o.c.

1/4" S.S. EDGE BAR, TYP. 3
SIDES EA. PIECE

HATCH COVER
SHOWN IN
OPEN POSITION

TOP OF GRATE,

5/16" TWISTED
S.S. CROSS
BARS at 4" o.c.

FIRST GALLERY LEVEL HATCH GRATE
SCALE: 3" = 1'-0"   PROPOSED FOR 1982 RESTORATION.

5/16" TWISTED S.S. CROSSBARS
at 4" o.c.

1-1/2" x 1/4" S.S. BEARING BARS at
1 3/8" o.c.

1/4" S.S. EDGE BAR
TYP. 3 SIDES EA. PIECE

2 PIECE GRATING

WROUGHT IRON ASTRAGAL

BASE GUTTER (INTEGRAL WITH
THE CAST IRON DECK)

COPPER ALLOY SCREWS

COPPER ALLOY VENT SHUTTERS
COPPER ALLOY VENT BASEPLATE

COPPER ALLOY
BASE TRANSOM

COPPER ALLOY
BOLTS & SCREWS

COPPER ALLOY
TRANSOM CLEAT

GALLERY DECK,
CONTINUOUS CAST IRON

LANTERN BASE VENTILATOR

SECOND GALLERY SECTION
SCALE: 6" = 1'-0"

NOTE: UNDERLINED NOTES PERTAIN TO 1982
RESTORATION.

GALLERY BRACKETS

COPPER ALLOY
NUTS & BOLTS

LOWER RAIL—
CAST IRON

CAST IRON POSTS
WITH ATTACHED LUGS

SECTION OF VENT BASEPLATE & SHUTTER
SCALE: 6" = 1'-0"

COPPER ALLOY-
SHUTTER

BASEPLATE-
COPPER ALLOY

SHUTTER

BASEPLATE

OPEN   CLOSE

PLAN OF VENT BASEPLATE & SHUTTER
SCALE: 6" = 1'-0"

NOTE: VENT BASEPLATE &
SHUTTERS REPLACED IN 1982
RESTORATION.

COPPER ALLOY CAP

CAST IRON
UPPER RAIL

NOTE: VENT BASEPLATE &
SHUTTERS REPLACED AS NEEDED IN 1982
RESTORATION.

DRAWN BY: B. SANTOS

DENVER SERVICE CENTER
OFFICE OF ARCHEOLOGY AND HISTORIC PRESERVATION
UNDER DIRECTION OF THE NATIONAL PARK SERVICE,
UNITED STATES DEPARTMENT OF THE INTERIOR

NAME AND LOCATION OF STRUCTURE
POINT REYES LIGHTHOUSE
POINT REYES NATIONAL MONUMENT, MARIN COUNTY, CALIFORNIA

SURVEY NO.
CA-
2250

HISTORIC AMERICAN
BUILDINGS SURVEY
SHEET 4 OF 5 SHEETS

612/25,002

126

Kraig Anderson

HABS No. CA-2250-1

Despite facing extreme weather, the Point Reyes Lighthouse has remained a fixture on the California coast. The lighthouse even survived an earthquake in 1906, which shifted the entire Point Reyes peninsula 18' to the north.

In 2003, a renovation project made repairs to the lighthouse, the stairs, and surrounding buildings.

127

PORT MAHON LIGHTHOUSE

KENT COUNTY, DELAWARE
ORIGINAL LIGHTHOUSE BUILT IN 1831

Located at the juncture of the Mahon River and the Delaware Bay, the Port Mahon Lighthouse was built to protect commercial oyster fisherman from the dangerous shoals located just offshore. The lighthouse was an excellent example of screw pile architecture, a technique in which the lighthouse foundation is screwed directly into the ocean floor. This architectural technique, however, is very susceptible to the effects of erosion. Four lighthouses were built at Port Mahon. The first three, constructed in 1831, 1860, and 1875, were either taken down or moved when their unstable foundations made them unsafe. The fourth lighthouse was built in 1903. The building contained eleven rooms that were used to house the keeper, who attended the lighthouse's kerosene lantern, and his family. The lighthouse was automated in 1949. Left unattended, the building gradually fell into disrepair. It was destroyed in a fire in 1984, leaving only the foundation.

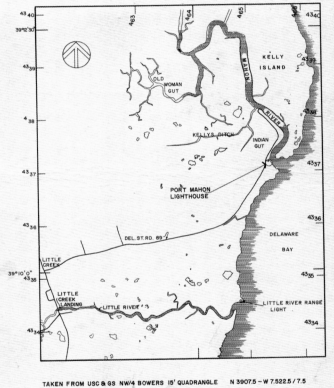

TAKEN FROM USC & GS NW/4 BOWERS 15' QUADRANGLE   N 3907.5 – W 7.522.5 / 7.5

LOCATION MAP   1"=1000.0'

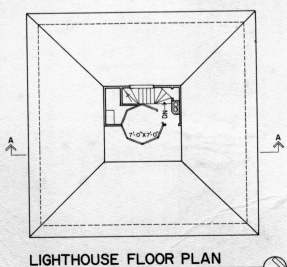

DN →

7'-0" X 7'-0"

A   A

LIGHTHOUSE FLOOR PLAN

MID-ATLANTIC REGION   PHILADELPHIA, PA.
OFFICE OF ARCHEOLOGY AND HISTORIC PRESERVATION
HERITAGE CONSERVATION AND RECREATION SERVICE
UNITED STATES DEPARTMENT OF THE INTERIOR

NAME AND LOCATION OF STRUCTURE
PORT MAHON LIGHTHOUSE
DELAWARE STATE ROAD 89 (LITTLE CREEK VICINITY) KENT COUNTY, DELAWARE

SURVEY NO.
DE-214

HISTORIC AMERICAN
BUILDINGS SURVEY
SHEET 1 OF 4 SHEETS

The Port Mahon Lighthouse was an important navigational point for fishermen on the Delaware Bay.

The Port Mahon Lighthouse sat at the juncture of the Mahon River and the Delaware Bay, guiding ships around dangerous shoals.

HABS No. DE-214-10

The keeper and his family lived in the lighthouse and attended the kerosene lantern.

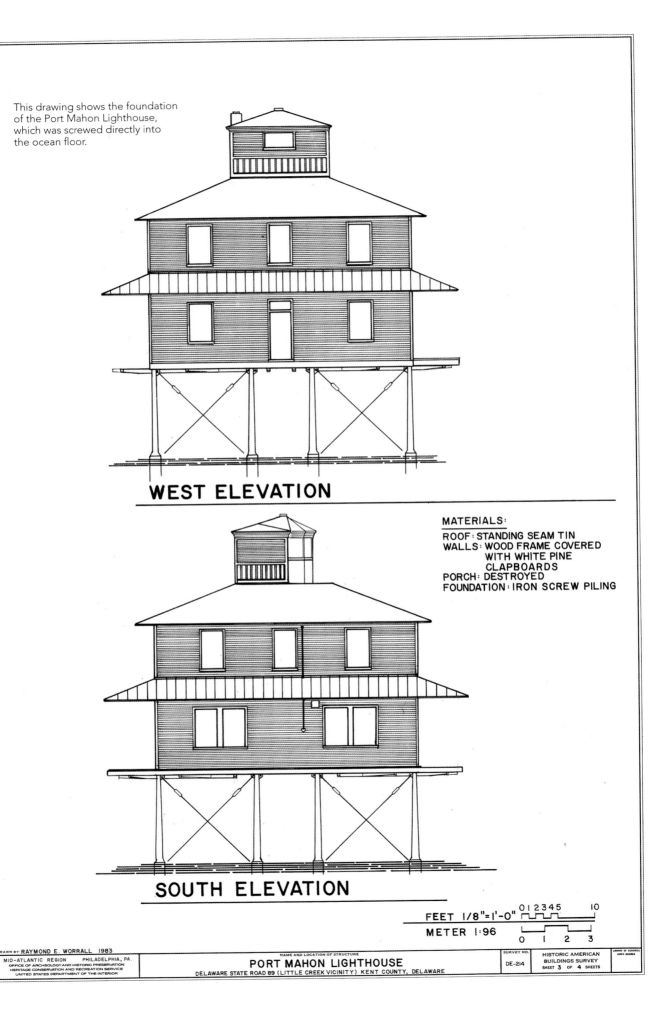

This drawing shows the foundation of the Port Mahon Lighthouse, which was screwed directly into the ocean floor.

WEST ELEVATION

SOUTH ELEVATION

MATERIALS:

ROOF: STANDING SEAM TIN
WALLS: WOOD FRAME COVERED
      WITH WHITE PINE
      CLAPBOARDS
PORCH: DESTROYED
FOUNDATION: IRON SCREW PILING

FEET 1/8"=1'-0" 0 1 2 3 4 5   10
METER 1:96 0 1 2 3

DRAWN BY RAYMOND E. WORRALL 1983

MID-ATLANTIC REGION   PHILADELPHIA, PA.
OFFICE OF ARCHEOLOGY AND HISTORIC PRESERVATION
HERITAGE CONSERVATION AND RECREATION SERVICE
UNITED STATES DEPARTMENT OF THE INTERIOR

NAME AND LOCATION OF STRUCTURE
PORT MAHON LIGHTHOUSE
DELAWARE STATE ROAD 89 (LITTLE CREEK VICINITY) KENT COUNTY, DELAWARE

SURVEY NO.
DE-214

HISTORIC AMERICAN
BUILDINGS SURVEY
SHEET 3 OF 4 SHEETS

LIBRARY OF CONGRESS

The lighthouse exterior
is shown here.

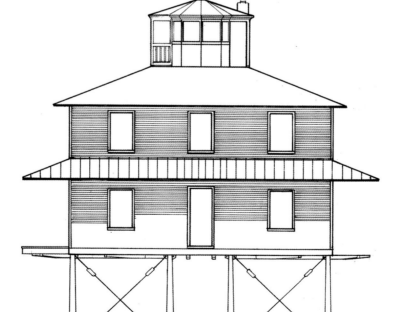

NORTH ELEVATION

EAST ELEVATION

DRAWN BY: RAYMOND E. WORRALL 1983

MID-ATLANTIC REGION   PHILADELPHIA, PA.
OFFICE OF ARCHEOLOGY AND HISTORIC PRESERVATION
HERITAGE CONSERVATION AND RECREATION SERVICE
UNITED STATES DEPARTMENT OF THE INTERIOR

NAME AND LOCATION OF STRUCTURE
PORT MAHON LIGHTHOUSE
DELAWARE STATE ROAD 89 (LITTLE CREEK VICINITY) KENT COUNTY, DELAWARE

SURVEY NO.
DE-214

HISTORIC AMERICAN
BUILDINGS SURVEY
SHEET 3 OF 4 SHEETS

LIBRARY OF CONGRESS
INDEX NUMBER

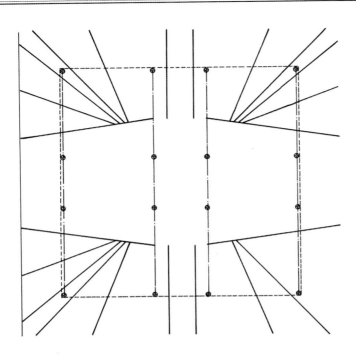

CANTILEVERED DECK FRAMING PLAN

MATERIALS:

FOUNDATION: IRON SCREW PILE

DECK FRAMING: WOOD BEAMS

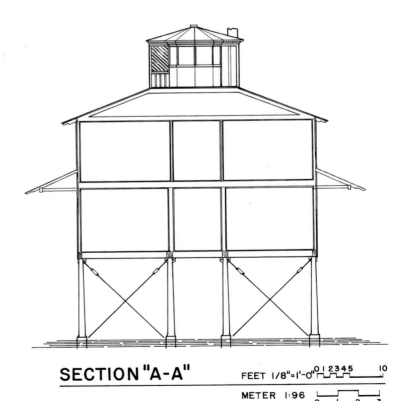

SECTION "A-A"

FEET 1/8"=1'-0"   0 1 2 3 4 5   10

METER 1:96   0 1 2 3

MATERIALS:

FOUNDATION: IRON SCREW PILE

WALLS: WOOD WITH WHITE PINE
         CLAPBOARDS

ROOF: WOOD WITH STANDING SEAM
      TIN

The details of the lighthouse deck are featured on this drawing.

DRAWN BY: RAYMOND E. WORRALL 1983

MID-ATLANTIC REGION   PHILADELPHIA, PA.
OFFICE OF ARCHEOLOGY AND HISTORIC PRESERVATION
HERITAGE CONSERVATION AND RECREATION SERVICE
UNITED STATES DEPARTMENT OF THE INTERIOR

NAME AND LOCATION OF STRUCTURE
PORT MAHON LIGHTHOUSE
DELAWARE STATE ROAD 89 (LITTLE CREEK VICINITY) KENT COUNTY, DELAWARE

SURVEY NO.
DE-214

HISTORIC AMERICAN
BUILDINGS SURVEY
SHEET 4 OF 4 SHEETS

LIBRARY OF CONGRESS
JAMES MONROE

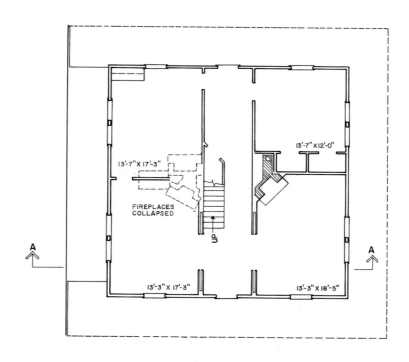

FIRST FLOOR PLAN

FEET 1/8"=1'-0"
0 1 2 3 4 5   10

0   1   2   3
METERS 1:96

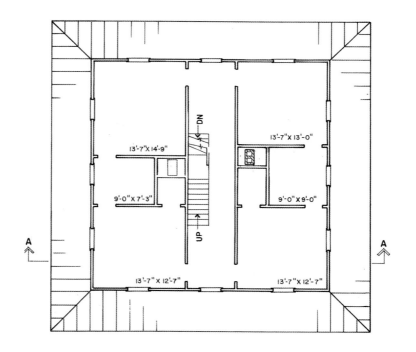

The images on this plan show the various floors of the Port Mahon Lighthouse.

SECOND FLOOR PLAN

DRAWN BY: RAYMOND E. WORRALL 1983

MID-ATLANTIC REGION   PHILADELPHIA, PA.
OFFICE OF ARCHEOLOGY AND HISTORIC PRESERVATION
HERITAGE CONSERVATION AND RECREATION SERVICE
UNITED STATES DEPARTMENT OF THE INTERIOR

NAME AND LOCATION OF STRUCTURE
PORT MAHON LIGHTHOUSE
DELAWARE STATE ROAD 89 (LITTLE CREEK VICINITY) KENT COUNTY, DELAWARE

SURVEY NO.
DE-214

HISTORIC AMERICAN
BUILDINGS SURVEY
SHEET 2 OF 4 SHEETS

The Port Mahon Lighthouse was automated in 1949 and subsequently abandoned. It quickly fell into disrepair.

In 1984, a fire destroyed the lighthouse building, leaving only the foundation behind.

PORTLAND BREAKWATER LIGHTHOUSE

CUMBERLAND COUNTY, MAINE
ORIGINAL LIGHTHOUSE BUILT IN 1855

The Portland Breakwater Lighthouse was constructed in 1855 after a breakwater was built to protect Portland Harbor from strong ocean waves. The lighthouse's fifth-order Fresnel lens produced a red light that marked the edge of the breakwater, allowing ships entering or leaving the harbor to steer around the structure. In 1873, an extension was added to the breakwater, and a new lighthouse was needed to indicate the end of the addition. In 1875, the second Portland Breakwater Lighthouse was completed. The new lighthouse was made of brick lined with cast iron. It is thought that Thomas Walter, an architect who worked on the United States capitol building, might have had something to do with the design of the lighthouse, due to the similar details included on the structure's exterior. In 1934, the lighthouse received an electric light, which was later deactivated in 1942. Since then, the lighthouse has been put on the National Register of Historic Places and has been relit.

138

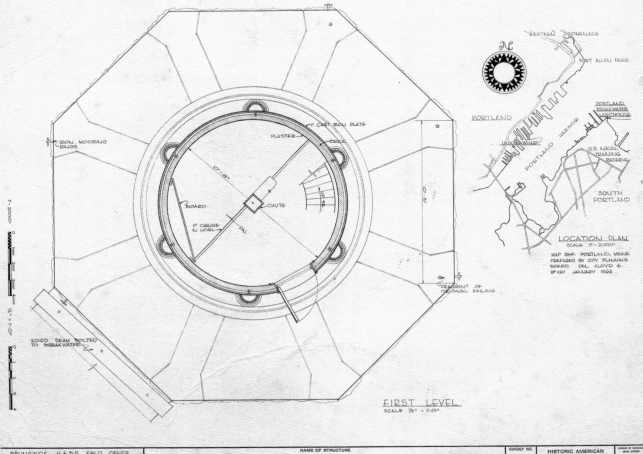

FIRST LEVEL
SCALE 1/2" = 1'-0"

LOCATION PLAN
SCALE 1" = 2000'
MAP REF: PORTLAND, MAINE
PREPARED BY CITY PLANNING
BOARD. DEL. FLOYD E.
McKAY JANUARY 1962

BRUNSWICK H.A.B.S. FIELD OFFICE
MAINE MID-COAST SURVEY II
UNDER DIRECTION OF UNITED STATES DEPARTMENT OF THE INTERIOR
NATIONAL PARK SERVICE, BRANCH OF PLANS AND DESIGN

NAME OF STRUCTURE
PORTLAND BREAKWATER LIGHTHOUSE
PORTLAND POINT   SOUTH PORTLAND   CUMBERLAND COUNTY   MAINE

SURVEY NO.
ME. 112

HISTORIC AMERICAN
BUILDINGS SURVEY
SHEET 1 OF 3 SHEETS

In 1836, construction began on a breakwater off the coast of Maine to help shelter Portland Harbor and ships anchored there from the damaging effects of strong ocean waves.

The plans for the breakwater called for a lighthouse to mark its location for ships entering or leaving the harbor. Too much money was spent building the breakwater, however, so a lighthouse was not completed at the site until 1855.

The original tower of the Portland Breakwater Lighthouse was a small octagonal structure about 25' tall.

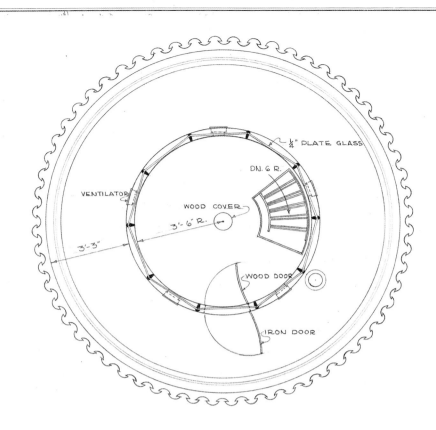

THIRD LEVEL
SCALE: ½" = 1'-0"

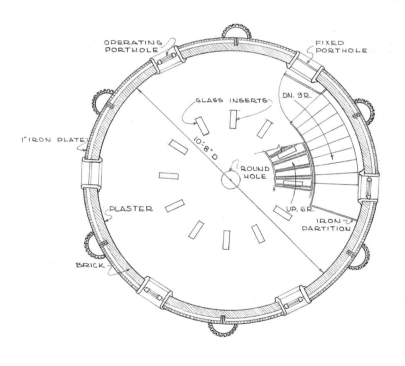

This plan shows the second and third levels of the lighthouse.

NORTH

SECOND LEVEL
SCALE: ½" = 1'-0"

½" = 1'-0"   0   1   2   3   4

DEL. W.G. BRAUN, 1962.

BRUNSWICK   H.A.B.S.   FIELD OFFICE
MAINE   MID-COAST   SURVEY II
UNDER DIRECTION OF UNITED STATES DEPARTMENT OF THE INTERIOR
NATIONAL PARK SERVICE, BRANCH OF PLANS AND DESIGN

NAME OF STRUCTURE
PORTLAND   BREAKWATER   LIGHTHOUSE
PORTLAND POINT   SOUTH PORTLAND   CUMBERLAND COUNTY   MAINE

SURVEY NO.
ME. 112

HISTORIC AMERICAN
BUILDINGS SURVEY
SHEET 2 OF 3 SHEETS

A second tower was built in 1875 after the breakwater was extended farther into the harbor.

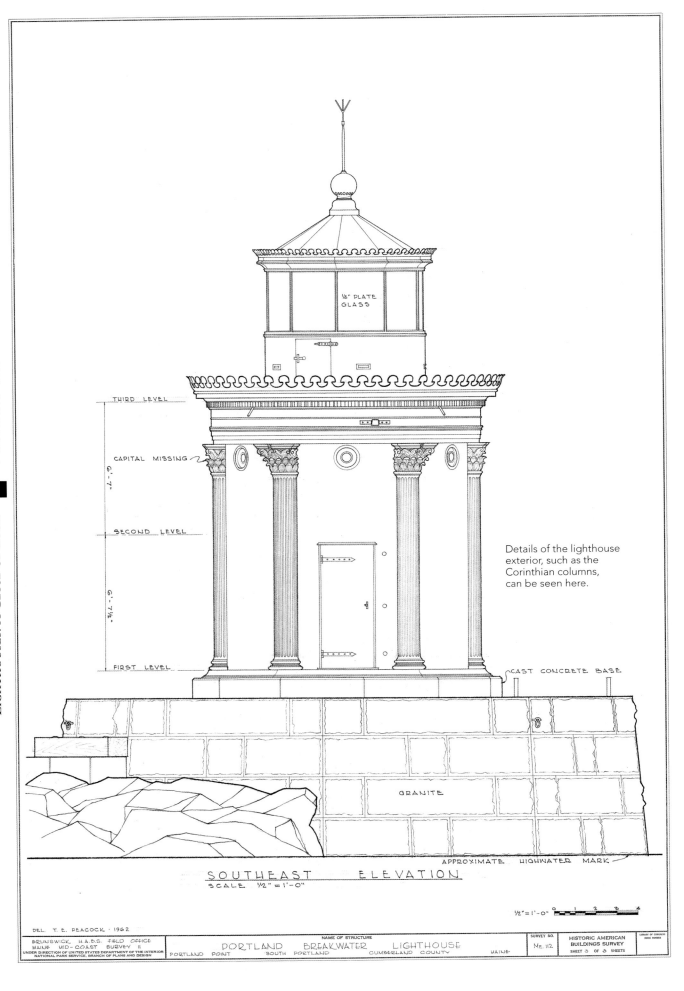

¼" PLATE GLASS

THIRD LEVEL

CAPITAL MISSING

6'-7"

SECOND LEVEL

6'-7½"

FIRST LEVEL

CAST CONCRETE BASE

Details of the lighthouse exterior, such as the Corinthian columns, can be seen here.

GRANITE

APPROXIMATE HIGHWATER MARK

SOUTHEAST ELEVATION
SCALE ½" = 1'-0"

½" = 1'-0" 0 1 2 3 4

DEL. T. E. PEACOCK · 1962

BRUNSWICK H.A.B.S. FIELD OFFICE
MAINE MID-COAST SURVEY II
UNDER DIRECTION OF UNITED STATES DEPARTMENT OF THE INTERIOR
NATIONAL PARK SERVICE, BRANCH OF PLANS AND DESIGN

NAME OF STRUCTURE
PORTLAND BREAKWATER LIGHTHOUSE
PORTLAND POINT   SOUTH PORTLAND   CUMBERLAND COUNTY   MAINE

SURVEY NO.
ME. 112

HISTORIC AMERICAN
BUILDINGS SURVEY
SHEET 3 OF 3 SHEETS

Although it cannot be proven, it is thought that Thomas Walter, one of the architects who worked on the United States capitol building, might have influenced the design of the 1875 breakwater lighthouse.

145

146

The National Register of Historic
Places added the Portland Breakwater
Lighthouse to its list in 1973.

Kraig Anderson

This photo clearly shows the decorative architectural details found on the current Portland Breakwater Lighthouse, which are similar to those seen on the exterior of the United States capitol building.

Presque Isle Light Station

PRESQUE ISLE COUNTY, MICHIGAN
ORIGINAL LIGHTHOUSE BUILT IN 1839

Presque Isle, meaning "almost an island" in French, is a small section of land that juts out from the shore of Michigan into Lake Huron. A small harbor located at the south end of the isle often provided shelter for ships and other travelers. Traffic in and around the harbor increased in the 1830s, as many steam-powered vessels made it a fuel stop. The harbor was also frequently used as a shelter for ships during heavy storms. In 1839, construction began on a 30' tower that would mark the entrance to the harbor. The lighthouse was originally lit with a Lewis lamp that was replaced by a fourth-order Fresnel lens in 1857. By the 1860s, the keeper's house had fallen into such a dismal state that plans were made to replace it. The United States Lighthouse Board, however, soon proposed deactivating the lighthouse and building a taller structure at the north end of the isle to guide ships around it. A pair of range lights would be erected near the original lighthouse to help vessels navigate into the harbor. Construction on the range lights was completed in 1870, and the new lighthouse tower was finished in 1871. The new tower was 113' tall and housed a third-order Fresnel lens until it was automated in 1970. The old lighthouse was restored in the 1950s and opened as a museum in the 1960s. The photos featured here show the second lighthouse, which was completed in 1871.

The original Presque Isle Light Station was a small 30' tower that marked the entrance to the Presque Isle Harbor.

In the late 1800s, it was discovered that the keeper's quarters were unusable and needed to be rebuilt.

151

Instead of rebuilding at the original lighthouse location, however, the United States Lighthouse Board suggested building a new taller light at the opposite end of Presque Isle and a pair of range lights near the harbor.

The new tower would help guide ships around Presque Isle, a section of land that jutted out from mainland Michigan, while the range lights would serve to guide them into the harbor.

152

Jeff Rozema

The new tower is 113' tall and contained a third-order
Fresnel lens until the light was automated in 1970.

REEDY ISLAND RANGE REAR LIGHT

NEW CASTLE COUNTY, DELAWARE
BUILT IN 1910

Range lights were commonly used along the Delaware Bay to guide mariners into the bay's main channel. The range lights were operated in pairs with a small light located on the bank and a taller structure built much further inland. Sailors entering the bay would align their ships with the lights so that they saw one shining right on top of the other. As long as the lights were aligned in this way, sailors knew that their vessel was travelling toward the bay's main channel and was safe from islands and shoals. The Reedy Island Range Rear Light was built to mark a new channel that had been dredged in the bay near Philadelphia. The front light was placed between the Appoquinimink River and Blackbird Creek, while the rear light was built about 5,000 yards away near Taylors Bridge. Because it would take time to build a tower for the rear light, a temporary light that consisted of a wooden pole and a large headlight like those used on trains was put in place. In 1910, the iron tower was completed, and the fifth-order range rear lens was lit.

154

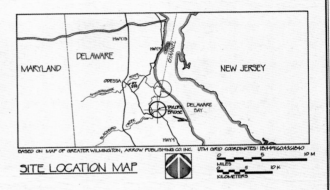

BASED ON MAP OF GREATER WILMINGTON, ARROW PUBLISHING CO. INC.   UTM GRID COORDINATES: 18.449160.4361840

SITE LOCATION MAP

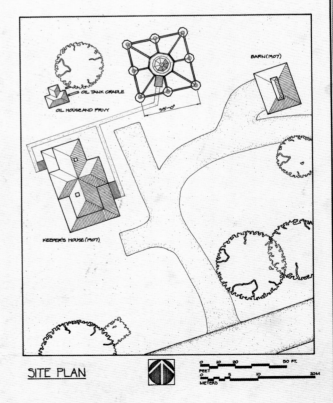

SITE PLAN

DELINEATED BY: DAVID PACKARD, 1976

STATE OF DELAWARE SURVEY
OFFICE OF ARCHEOLOGY AND HISTORIC PRESERVATION
NATIONAL PARK SERVICE
UNITED STATES DEPARTMENT OF THE INTERIOR

TAYLORS BRIDGE

REEDY ISLAND RANGE REAR LIGHT, 1910
NORTH SIDE OF HIGHWAY 9 AS THE HIGHWAY ENTERS TAYLORS BRIDGE
NEW CASTLE COUNTY   DELAWARE

SHEET
1 OF 2

HISTORIC AMERICAN
ENGINEERING RECORD
DE-11

IF REPRODUCED, PLEASE CREDIT: HISTORIC AMERICAN ENGINEERING RECORD, NATIONAL PARK SERVICE, NAME OF DELINEATOR, DATE OF THE DRAWING

The exterior structure of the lighthouse is shown here, featuring the cables and joints used to support the tower.

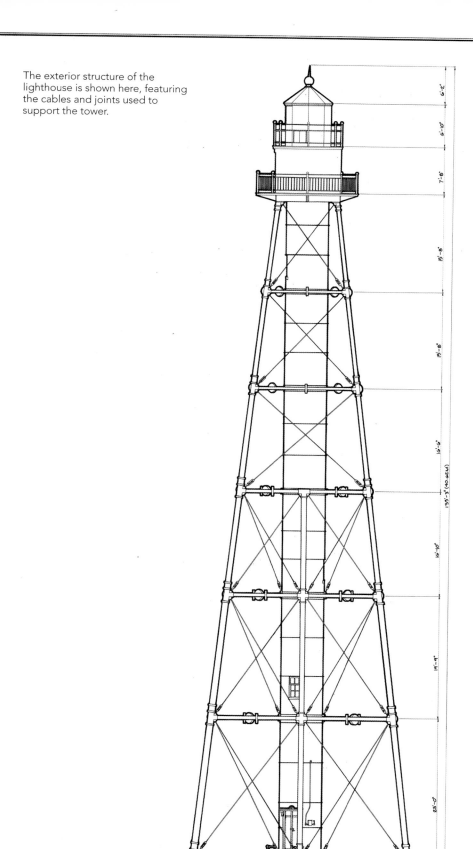

DELINEATED BY: DAVID PACKARD, 1976

STATE OF DELAWARE SURVEY
OFFICE OF ARCHEOLOGY AND HISTORIC PRESERVATION
NATIONAL PARK SERVICE
UNITED STATES DEPARTMENT OF THE INTERIOR

TAYLORS BRIDGE

REEDY ISLAND RANGE REAR LIGHT, 1910
NORTH SIDE OF HIGHWAY 9 AS THE HIGHWAY ENTERS TAYLORS BRIDGE
NEW CASTLE COUNTY
DELAWARE

SHEET
1 OF 2

HISTORIC AMERICAN
ENGINEERING RECORD
DE-11

IF REPRODUCED, PLEASE CREDIT: HISTORIC AMERICAN ENGINEERING RECORD, NATIONAL PARK SERVICE, NAME OF DELINEATOR, DATE OF THE DRAWING

The Reedy Island Range
Rear Light is used to guide
ships along the main channel
of the Delaware Bay.

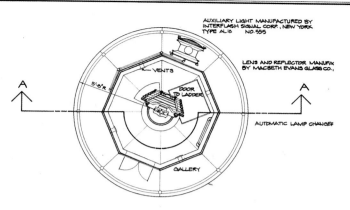

LANTERN ROOM PLAN

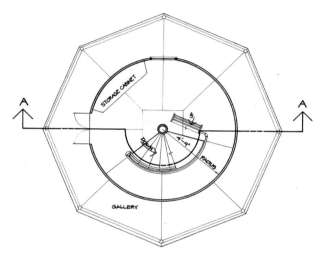

WATCHROOM PLAN

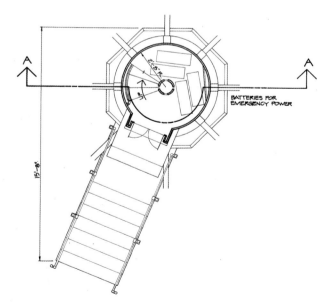

This drawing shows the interior layout of the lighthouse and features cutaway images of several upper levels.

ENTRANCE PLAN

DELINEATED BY: DAVID PACKARD, 1976

STATE OF DELAWARE SURVEY
OFFICE OF ARCHEOLOGY AND HISTORIC PRESERVATION
NATIONAL PARK SERVICE
UNITED STATES DEPARTMENT OF THE INTERIOR

TAYLORS BRIDGE

REEDY ISLAND RANGE REAR LIGHT, 1910
NORTH SIDE OF HIGHWAY 9 AS THE HIGHWAY ENTERS TAYLORS BRIDGE
NEW CASTLE COUNTY
DELAWARE

SHEET
2 OF 2

HISTORIC AMERICAN
ENGINEERING RECORD

DE-11

The rear light is actually part of a pair. A shorter front light is located much closer to the shore of the bay.

The range rear light is about 125' tall and contains a spiral staircase enclosed by cast iron walls.

HAER DE-11-4

The tower utilizes these structural supports to hold the weight of the cast iron used for construction.

These intricate joints, used in the
construction of the Reedy Island
Range Rear Light, allow the tower
to stand more than 100' tall so
its light can be seen by sailors on
the bay.

ROCK HARBOR LIGHTHOUSE

KEWEENAW COUNTY, MICHIGAN
BUILT IN 1856

Rock Harbor Lighthouse is the oldest of three lighthouses erected to aide navigation around Isle Royale in Lake Superior. Located about 14 miles away from the Canadian border, Isle Royale became a huge mining center in the 1840s, with more than a dozen mining companies taking up residence on the island. This boom in the mining industry led to increased ship traffic to and from the island, making a lighthouse a necessity. Construction began on Rock Harbor's 50' tower in 1855. The lighthouse's fourth-order Fresnel lens helped ships navigate the shoals of the Middle Passage, bringing them safely into the harbor. Shortly after the lighthouse was built, the mining industry began to lag, causing a decrease in ship traffic. The light was extinguished in 1859, only to be relit in the summer of 1874 after the Civil War led to an increased interest in metals. The light shone for the last time in 1879, and the lighthouse is now part of the Isle Royale National Park.

162

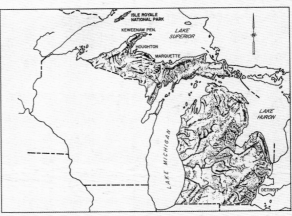

LOCATION MAP

PASSAGE ISLAND
PASSAGE ISLAND LIGHT STATION 1881

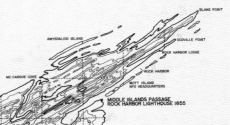

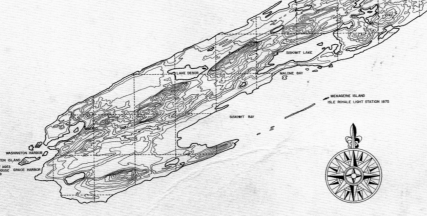

MILES
KILOMETERS

DRAWN BY: DAVID E. NAILL
ISLE ROYALE LIGHT STATIONS PROJECT
SUMMER 1992
NATIONAL PARK SERVICE
UNITED STATES DEPARTMENT OF THE INTERIOR

NAME AND LOCATION OF STRUCTURE
ROCK HARBOR LIGHTHOUSE
ISLE ROYALE NATIONAL PARK   COPPER HARBOR VICINITY   KEWEENAW COUNTY   MICHIGAN

SURVEY NO.
MI-386

HISTORIC AMERICAN BUILDINGS SURVEY
SHEET 1 OF 7 SHEETS

The Rock Harbor Lighthouse is the oldest of three lighthouses used to help ships navigate around Isle Royale.

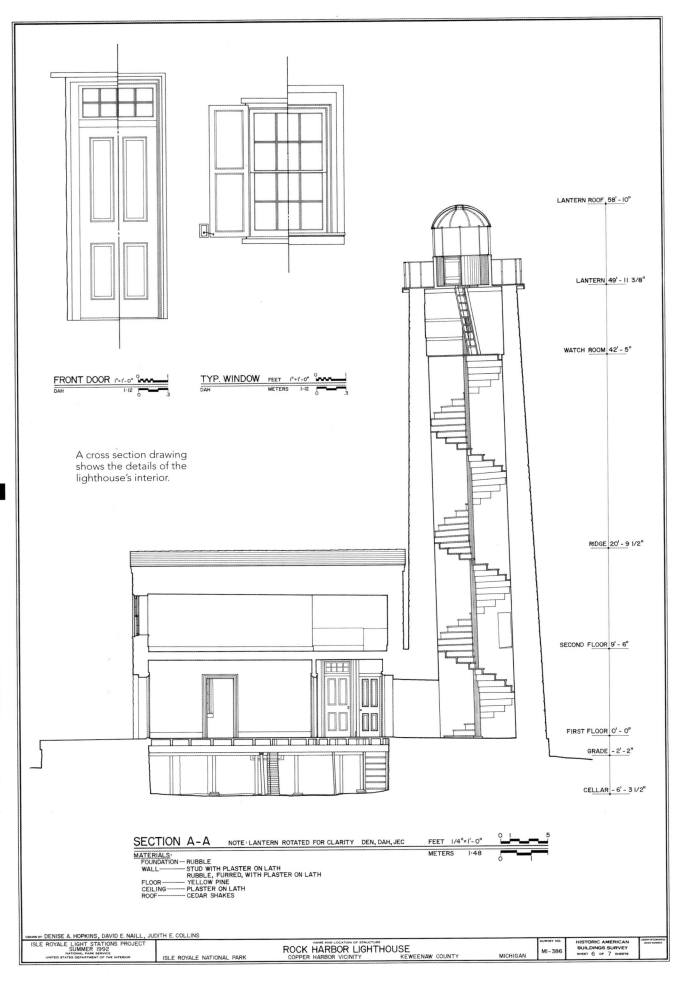

FRONT DOOR 1"=1'-0" 0

DAH 1:12 .3

TYP. WINDOW FEET 1"=1'-0" 0

DAH METERS 1:12 0 .3

A cross section drawing shows the details of the lighthouse's interior.

LANTERN ROOF 58'-10"

LANTERN 49'-11 3/8"

WATCH ROOM 42'-5"

RIDGE 20'-9 1/2"

SECOND FLOOR 9'-6"

FIRST FLOOR 0'-0"

GRADE -2'-2"

CELLAR -6'-3 1/2"

SECTION A-A NOTE: LANTERN ROTATED FOR CLARITY DEN, DAH, JEC FEET 1/4"=1'-0" 0 1 5

METERS 1:48 0 1

MATERIALS:
FOUNDATION — RUBBLE
WALL — STUD WITH PLASTER ON LATH
RUBBLE, FURRED, WITH PLASTER ON LATH
FLOOR — YELLOW PINE
CEILING — PLASTER ON LATH
ROOF — CEDAR SHAKES

DRAWN BY: DENISE A. HOPKINS, DAVID E. NAILL, JUDITH E. COLLINS

ISLE ROYALE LIGHT STATIONS PROJECT
SUMMER 1992
NATIONAL PARK SERVICE
UNITED STATES DEPARTMENT OF THE INTERIOR

NAME AND LOCATION OF STRUCTURE
ROCK HARBOR LIGHTHOUSE
ISLE ROYALE NATIONAL PARK   COPPER HARBOR VICINITY   KEWEENAW COUNTY   MICHIGAN

SURVEY NO.
MI-386

HISTORIC AMERICAN
BUILDINGS SURVEY
SHEET 6 OF 7 SHEETS

LIBRARY OF CONGRESS
INDEX NUMBER

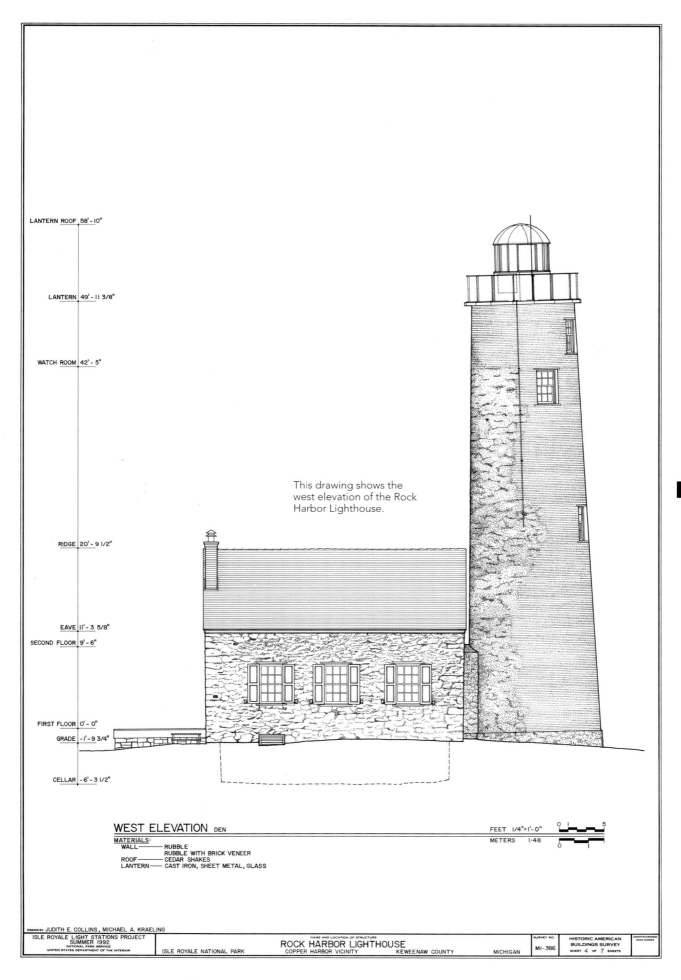

LANTERN ROOF 58'- 10"

LANTERN 49'- 11 3/8"

WATCH ROOM 42'- 5"

This drawing shows the west elevation of the Rock Harbor Lighthouse.

RIDGE 20'- 9 1/2"

EAVE 11'- 3 5/8"
SECOND FLOOR 9'- 6"

FIRST FLOOR 0'- 0"
GRADE -1'- 9 3/4"

CELLAR -6'- 3 1/2"

WEST ELEVATION DEN

FEET 1/4"=1'-0"
METERS 1:48

0 1 5

0 1

MATERIALS:
WALL ———— RUBBLE
            RUBBLE WITH BRICK VENEER
ROOF ———— CEDAR SHAKES
LANTERN —— CAST IRON, SHEET METAL, GLASS

DRAWN BY: JUDITH E. COLLINS, MICHAEL A. KRAELING

ISLE ROYALE LIGHT STATIONS PROJECT
SUMMER 1992
NATIONAL PARK SERVICE
UNITED STATES DEPARTMENT OF THE INTERIOR

NAME AND LOCATION OF STRUCTURE
ROCK HARBOR LIGHTHOUSE
ISLE ROYALE NATIONAL PARK   COPPER HARBOR VICINITY   KEWEENAW COUNTY   MICHIGAN

SURVEY NO.
MI-386

HISTORIC AMERICAN
BUILDINGS SURVEY
SHEET 4 OF 7 SHEETS

LIBRARY OF CONGRESS
INDEX NUMBER

The plans for the cellar and first floor of the keeper's quarters are shown here.

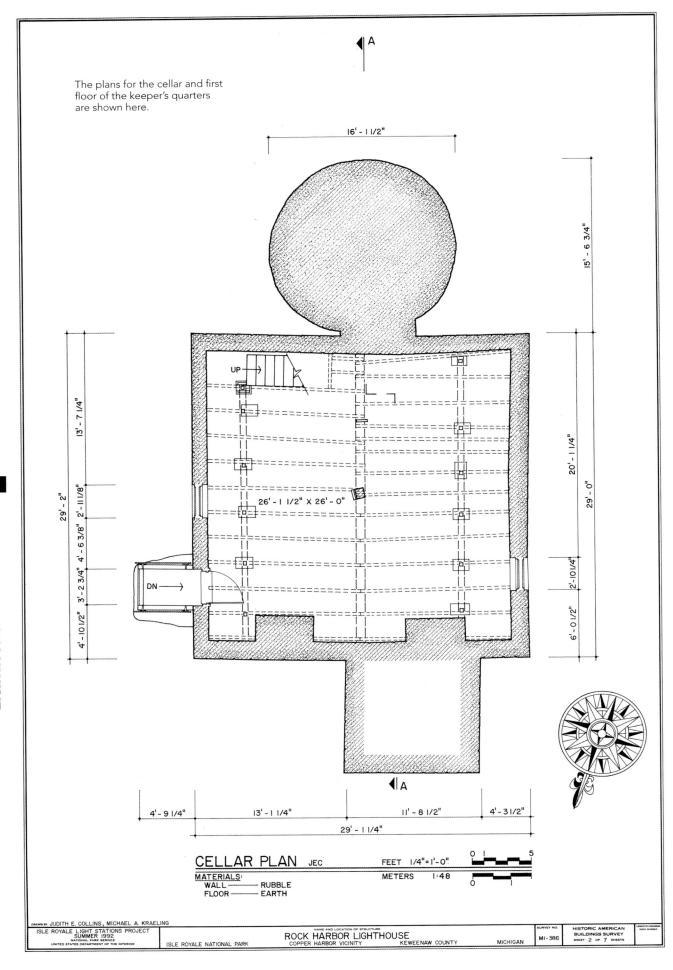

16' - 1 1/2"

15' - 6 3/4"

13' - 7 1/4"

2' - 11 1/8"

4' - 6 3/8"

3' - 2 3/4"

4' - 10 1/2"

29' - 2"

UP →

DN →

26' - 1 1/2" X 26' - 0"

20' - 1 1/4"

29' - 0"

2' - 10 1/4"

6' - 0 1/2"

4' - 9 1/4"   13' - 1 1/4"   11' - 8 1/2"   4' - 3 1/2"

29' - 11 1/4"

A

A

CELLAR PLAN   JEC

MATERIALS:
WALL ——— RUBBLE
FLOOR ——— EARTH

FEET   1/4" = 1'-0".

METERS   1:48

0   1   5

0   1

DRAWN BY: JUDITH E. COLLINS, MICHAEL A. KRAELING

ISLE ROYALE LIGHT STATIONS PROJECT
SUMMER 1992
NATIONAL PARK SERVICE
UNITED STATES DEPARTMENT OF THE INTERIOR

NAME AND LOCATION OF STRUCTURE
ROCK HARBOR LIGHTHOUSE
ISLE ROYALE NATIONAL PARK   COPPER HARBOR VICINITY   KEWEENAW COUNTY   MICHIGAN

SURVEY NO.
MI-386

HISTORIC AMERICAN
BUILDINGS SURVEY
SHEET 2 OF 7 SHEETS

LIBRARY OF CONGRESS
INDEX NUMBER

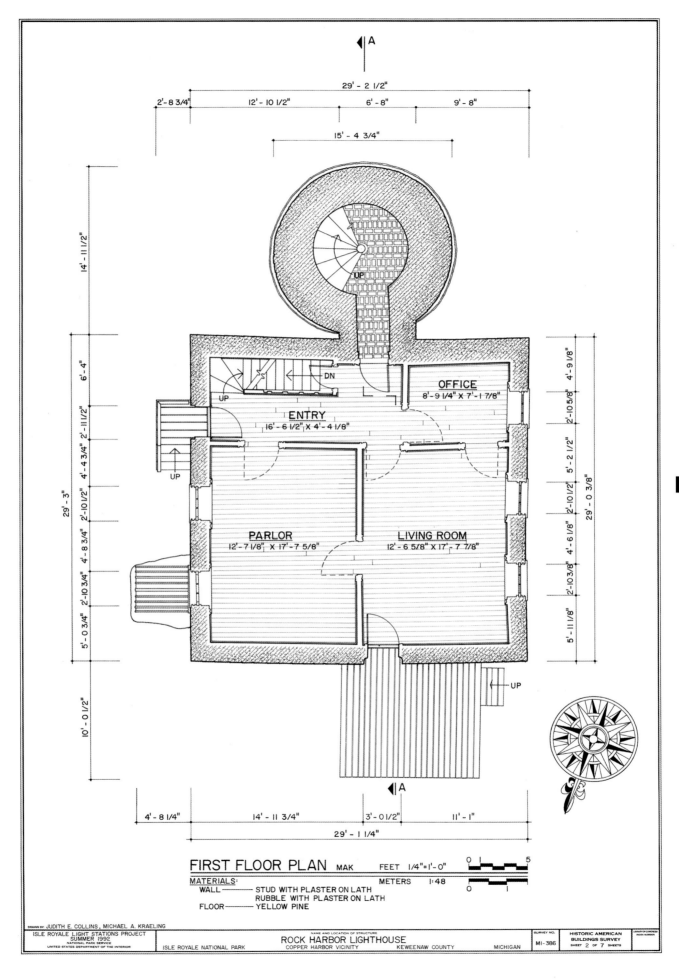

A

29' - 2 1/2"

2'- 8 3/4"   12'- 10 1/2"   6'- 8"   9'- 8"

15'- 4 3/4"

14'- 11 1/2"

6'- 4"

4'- 9 1/8"

2'-10 5/8"

2'-11 1/2"

5'- 2 1/2"

4'- 4 3/4"

29' - 3"

2'-10 1/2"

2'-10 1/2"

4'- 8 3/4"

4'- 6 1/8"

2'-10 3/4"

29'- 0 3/8"

5'- 0 3/4"

5'- 11 1/8"

10'- 0 1/2"

OFFICE
8'- 9 1/4" X 7'- 1 7/8"

DN

UP

ENTRY
16'- 6 1/2" X 4'- 4 1/8"

UP

UP

PARLOR
12'- 7 1/8" X 17'- 7 5/8"

LIVING ROOM
12'- 6 5/8" X 17'- 7 7/8"

UP

4'- 8 1/4"   14'- 11 3/4"   3'- 0 1/2"   11'- 1"

29' - 1 1/4"

A

FIRST FLOOR PLAN   MAK   FEET 1/4"=1'-0"

0   1   5

MATERIALS:
WALL ——— STUD WITH PLASTER ON LATH
           RUBBLE WITH PLASTER ON LATH
FLOOR ——— YELLOW PINE

METERS   1:48

0   1

DRAWN BY: JUDITH E. COLLINS, MICHAEL A. KRAELING

ISLE ROYALE LIGHT STATIONS PROJECT
SUMMER 1992
NATIONAL PARK SERVICE
UNITED STATES DEPARTMENT OF THE INTERIOR   ISLE ROYALE NATIONAL PARK

NAME AND LOCATION OF STRUCTURE

ROCK HARBOR LIGHTHOUSE
COPPER HARBOR VICINITY   KEWEENAW COUNTY   MICHIGAN

SURVEY NO.
MI-386

HISTORIC AMERICAN
BUILDINGS SURVEY
SHEET 2 OF 7 SHEETS

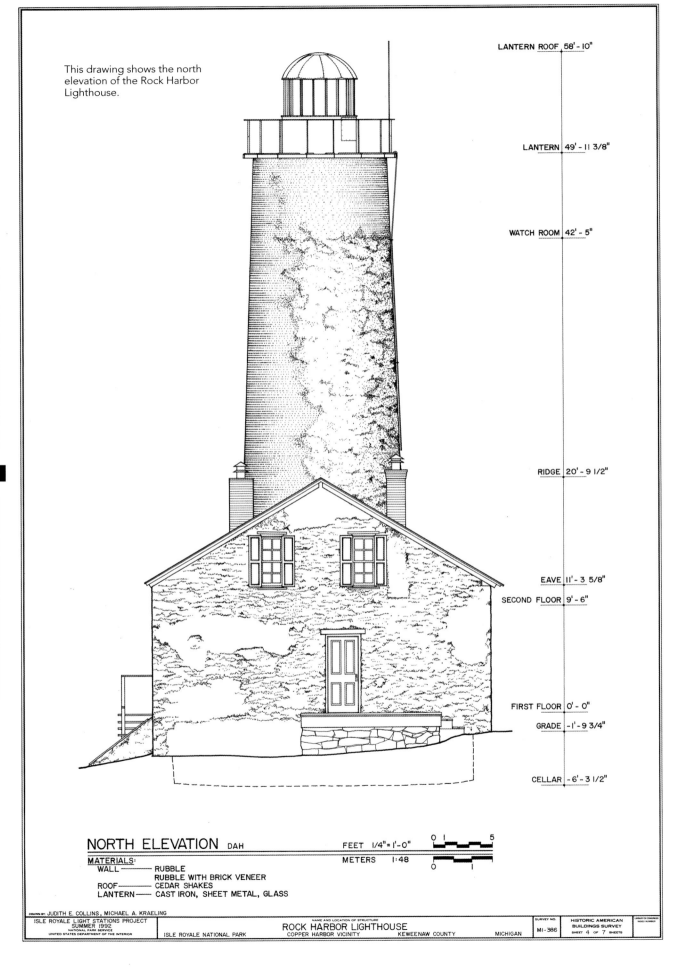

This drawing shows the north elevation of the Rock Harbor Lighthouse.

LANTERN ROOF 58' - 10"

LANTERN 49' - 11 3/8"

WATCH ROOM 42' - 5"

RIDGE 20' - 9 1/2"

EAVE 11' - 3 5/8"

SECOND FLOOR 9' - 6"

FIRST FLOOR 0' - 0"

GRADE -1' - 9 3/4"

CELLAR -6' - 3 1/2"

NORTH ELEVATION DAH

FEET 1/4" = 1'-0"

METERS 1:48

0 1 5

0 1

MATERIALS:
WALL ———— RUBBLE
          RUBBLE WITH BRICK VENEER
ROOF———— CEDAR SHAKES
LANTERN—— CAST IRON, SHEET METAL, GLASS

DRAWN BY: JUDITH E. COLLINS, MICHAEL A. KRAELING

ISLE ROYALE LIGHT STATIONS PROJECT
SUMMER 1992
NATIONAL PARK SERVICE
UNITED STATES DEPARTMENT OF THE INTERIOR

ISLE ROYALE NATIONAL PARK

NAME AND LOCATION OF STRUCTURE
ROCK HARBOR LIGHTHOUSE
COPPER HARBOR VICINITY   KEWEENAW COUNTY   MICHIGAN

SURVEY NO.
MI-386

HISTORIC AMERICAN
BUILDINGS SURVEY
SHEET 4 OF 7 SHEETS

The Rock Harbor Lighthouse is now part of the Isle Royale National Park.

ROCK OF AGES LIGHTHOUSE

KEWEENAW COUNTY, MICHIGAN
BUILT IN 1908

The Rock of Ages Lighthouse was built on a rock about 50' wide and 210' long, located 2.5 miles off the shore of Isle Royale in Lake Superior. Although very few wrecks had occurred on the rock and the surrounding reef, toward the end of the 1800s, many ships travelling to Duluth began to cut closer to Isle Royale and the hazardous rock. It was decided that a lighthouse should be built to prevent potential collisions in the future. Building the lighthouse on the remote rock presented a challenge. A temporary work station was set up on Isle Royale until construction progressed far enough to allow work crews to live on the rock. When the lighthouse was completed, it stood ten stories tall, consisting of a two-story concrete cellar, and eight upper stories that were made of brick built around a steel infrastructure. At the time, the construction of the lighthouse was considered an engineering feat. Due to budgetary concerns, the tower's second-order Fresnel lens was not installed until 1910. The light was placed in mercury to help support its weight, and a clockwork system was used to turn it. The lighthouse became automated in 1985 and is still active today. The original Fresnel lens can be seen on Isle Royal at the Windigo Visitors Center.

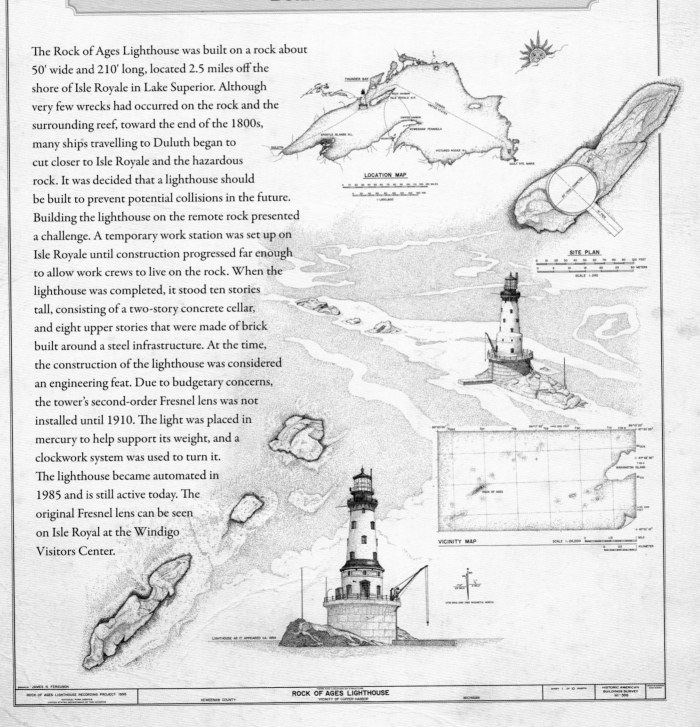

LOCATION MAP

SITE PLAN
SCALE 1:240

VICINITY MAP   SCALE 1:24,000

LIGHTHOUSE AS IT APPEARED CA. 1954

UTM GRID AND 1985 MAGNETIC NORTH

DRAWN BY: JAMES N. FERGUSON
ROCK OF AGES LIGHTHOUSE RECORDING PROJECT 1995
NATIONAL PARK SERVICE
UNITED STATES DEPARTMENT OF THE INTERIOR

ROCK OF AGES LIGHTHOUSE
VICINITY OF COPPER HARBOR

KEEWEENAW COUNTY   MICHIGAN

SHEET 1 OF 10 SHEETS   HISTORIC AMERICAN
BUILDINGS SURVEY
MI-388

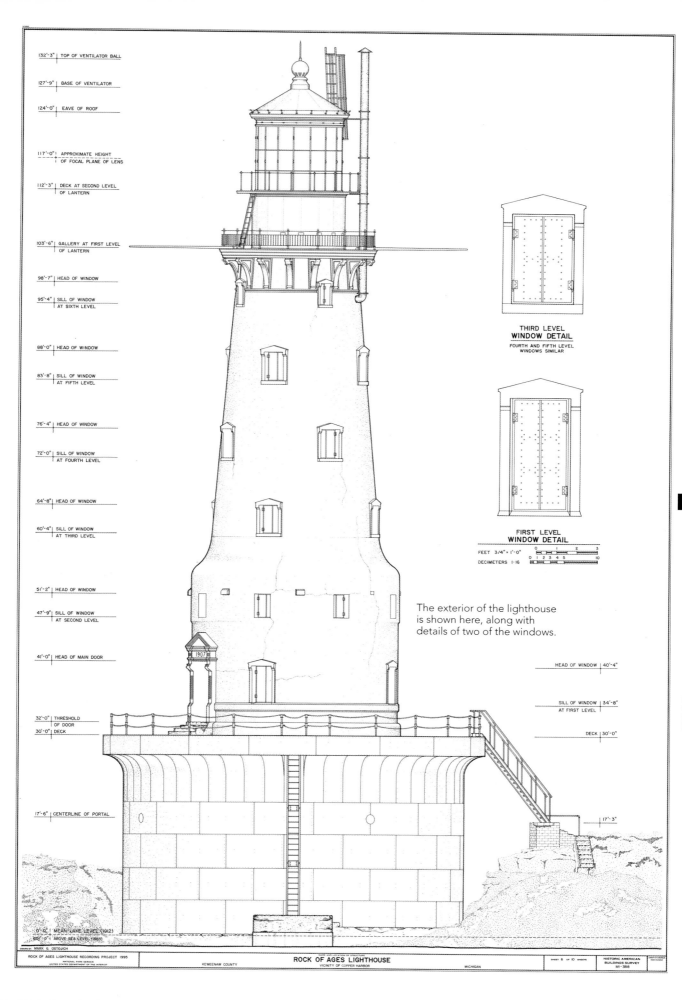

132'-3" TOP OF VENTILATOR BALL

127'-9" BASE OF VENTILATOR

124'-0" EAVE OF ROOF

117'-0" APPROXIMATE HEIGHT OF FOCAL PLANE OF LENS

112'-3" DECK AT SECOND LEVEL OF LANTERN

103'-6" GALLERY AT FIRST LEVEL OF LANTERN

98'-7" HEAD OF WINDOW

95'-4" SILL OF WINDOW AT SIXTH LEVEL

88'-0" HEAD OF WINDOW

83'-8" SILL OF WINDOW AT FIFTH LEVEL

76'-4" HEAD OF WINDOW

72'-0" SILL OF WINDOW AT FOURTH LEVEL

64'-8" HEAD OF WINDOW

60'-4" SILL OF WINDOW AT THIRD LEVEL

51'-2" HEAD OF WINDOW

47'-9" SILL OF WINDOW AT SECOND LEVEL

41'-0" HEAD OF MAIN DOOR

32'-0" THRESHOLD OF DOOR

30'-0" DECK

17'-6" CENTERLINE OF PORTAL

0'-0" MEAN LAKE LEVEL (1912)
601'-0" ABOVE SEA LEVEL (1985)

1907

THIRD LEVEL
WINDOW DETAIL
FOURTH AND FIFTH LEVEL WINDOWS SIMILAR

FIRST LEVEL
WINDOW DETAIL

FEET 3/4" = 1'-0"
DECIMETERS 1:16

The exterior of the lighthouse is shown here, along with details of two of the windows.

HEAD OF WINDOW 40'-4"

SILL OF WINDOW AT FIRST LEVEL 34'-8"

DECK 30'-0"

17'-3"

DRAWN BY: MARK G. OSTOJICH

ROCK OF AGES LIGHTHOUSE RECORDING PROJECT 1995
NATIONAL PARK SERVICE
UNITED STATES DEPARTMENT OF THE INTERIOR

KEWEENAW COUNTY

ROCK OF AGES LIGHTHOUSE
VICINITY OF COPPER HARBOR

MICHIGAN

SHEET 6 OF 10 SHEETS

HISTORIC AMERICAN BUILDINGS SURVEY
MI-388

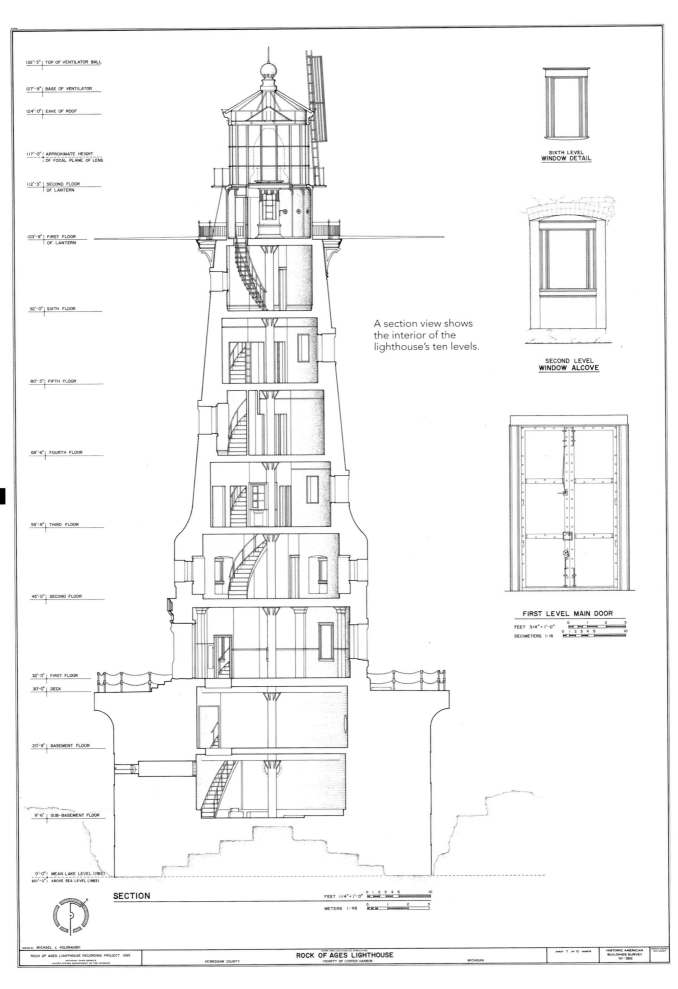

132'-3" TOP OF VENTILATOR BALL

127'-9" BASE OF VENTILATOR

124'-0" EAVE OF ROOF

117'-0" APPROXIMATE HEIGHT OF FOCAL PLANE OF LENS

112'-3" SECOND FLOOR OF LANTERN

103'-9" FIRST FLOOR OF LANTERN

92'-0" SIXTH FLOOR

80'-3" FIFTH FLOOR

68'-6" FOURTH FLOOR

56'-9" THIRD FLOOR

45'-0" SECOND FLOOR

32'-0" FIRST FLOOR

30'-0" DECK

20'-9" BASEMENT FLOOR

9'-6" SUB-BASEMENT FLOOR

0'-0" MEAN LAKE LEVEL (1912)

601'-0" ABOVE SEA LEVEL (1983)

SECTION

FEET 1/4" = 1'-0"

METERS 1:48

SIXTH LEVEL
WINDOW DETAIL

SECOND LEVEL
WINDOW ALCOVE

A section view shows the interior of the lighthouse's ten levels.

FIRST LEVEL MAIN DOOR

FEET 3/4" = 1'-0"

DECIMETERS 1:16

DRAWN BY: MICHAEL J. KOLONAUSKI

ROCK OF AGES LIGHTHOUSE RECORDING PROJECT 1995
NATIONAL PARK SERVICE
UNITED STATES DEPARTMENT OF THE INTERIOR

ROCK OF AGES LIGHTHOUSE
VICINITY OF COPPER HARBOR
KEWEENAW COUNTY   MICHIGAN

SHEET 7 OF 10 SHEETS

HISTORIC AMERICAN
BUILDINGS SURVEY
MI-386

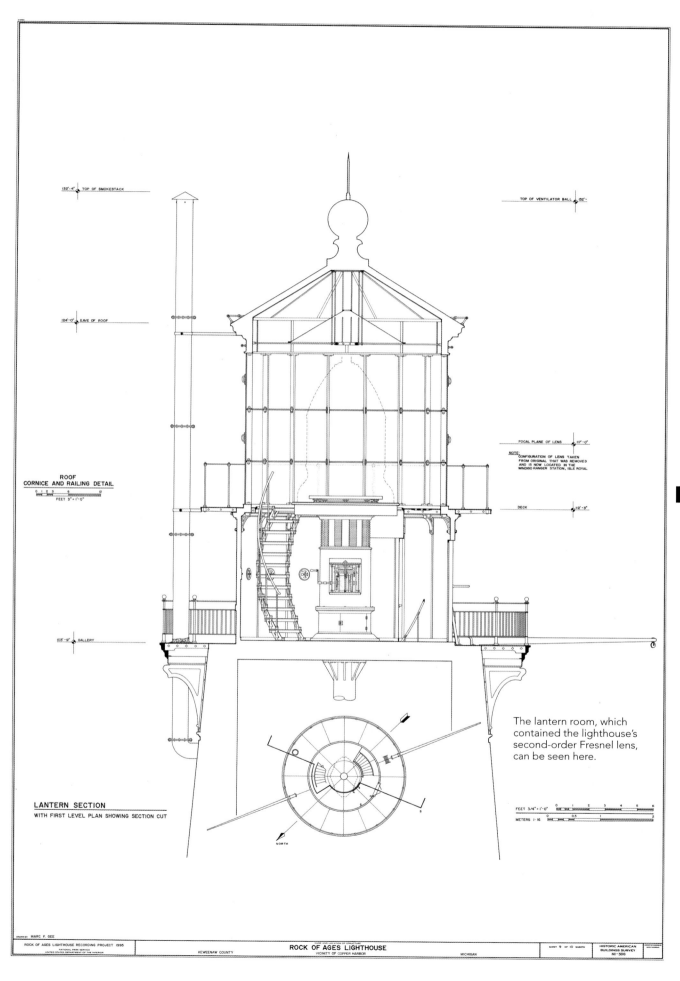

132'-4" TOP OF SMOKESTACK

TOP OF VENTILATOR BALL 132'-

124'-0" EAVE OF ROOF

FOCAL PLANE OF LENS 117'-0"

NOTE: CONFIGURATION OF LENS TAKEN FROM ORIGINAL THAT WAS REMOVED AND IS NOW LOCATED IN THE WINDIGO RANGER STATION, ISLE ROYAL

ROOF
CORNICE AND RAILING DETAIL

0 1 2 3   6   12
FEET 3" = 1'-0"

DECK 112'-3"

103'-9" GALLERY

The lantern room, which contained the lighthouse's second-order Fresnel lens, can be seen here.

LANTERN SECTION
WITH FIRST LEVEL PLAN SHOWING SECTION CUT

NORTH

FEET 3/4" = 1'-0"   0 1 2 3 4 5 6
METERS 1:16   0   0.5   1   2

DRAWN BY: MARC F. GEE

INDEX

Built in America Series

Discover America's rich architectural past.

Covered Bridges:
A Close-Up Look

A Tour of America's Iconic Architecture through Historic Photos and Detailed Drawings
By the Editors at Fox Chapel Publishing

Whether you are a casual explorer or a serious history buff, this glimpse into America's architectural past with hands-on GPS site coordinates and detailed architectural plans provides a vivid picture of covered bridges.

ISBN: 978-1-56523-561-8
$19.95 • 160 Pages

Coming Soon in the Series:

Barns: A Close-Up Look

A Tour of America's Iconic Architecture through Historic Photos and Detailed Drawings
By the Editors at Fox Chapel Publishing

ISBN: 978-1-56523-562-5
$19.95 • 128 Pages

Travel through the pages of these books to experience these great museums—the Smithsonian, Winterthur, and the Museum of the History of Science at Oxford University.

Studio Furniture of the Renwick Gallery
Smithsonian American Art Museum
By Oscar P. Fitzgerald

This absorbing volume features profiles and interviews of 64 artists – including Sam Maloof and James Krenov – that reveal artistic influences along with 112 stunning photos of iconic work.

ISBN: 978-1-56523-367-6
$35.00 • 224 pages

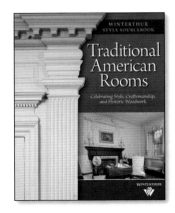

Traditional American Rooms
Celebrating Style, Craftsmanship, and Historic Woodwork
By Brent Hull and Christine G.H. Franck

Immerse yourself in the elegance and character of historic American architecture with this guide to the magnificent millwork of the Winterthur Museum and Country Estate.

ISBN: 978-1-56523-322-5
$35.00 • 184 Pages

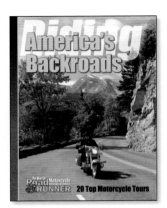

Riding America's Backroads
20 Top Motorcycle Tours
By Editors of RoadRUNNER Magazine

Tour America on two wheels with this fine assortment of writing and photography regularly featured in the pages of RoadRUNNER Motorcycle Touring & Travel magazine.

ISBN: 978-1-56523-479-6
$29.95 • 192 Pages

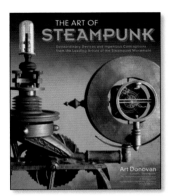

The Art of Steampunk
Extraordinary Devices and Ingenius Contraptions from the Leading Artists of the Steampunk Movement
By Art Donovan

Dive into the world of Steampunk where machines are functional pieces of art and the design is only as limited as the artist's imagination.

ISBN: 978-1-56523-573-1
$24.95 • 128 Pages